CONTENTS

ABBREVIATIONS

BMH	Bureau of Military History
GAA	Gaelic Athletic Association
GHQ	General Headquarters
GPA	Gaelic Players Association
IRA	Irish Republican Army
IRAO	Irish Republican Army Organisation
IRB	Irish Republican Brotherhood
NCO	Non-commissioned Officer
O/C	Officer Commanding
RIC	Royal Irish Constabulary
TD	Teachta Dála (member of Dáil Éireann)

ACKNOWLEDGEMENTS

I would like to thank the following:

The late Des Cox, Carrick-on-Shannnon, County Leitrim, for implanting the idea of writing the book.

The Bureau of Military History, Military Archives, Ireland. The book would not have been possible without access to the witness statements which are available on its website. Most of the material about Sam Maguire's work during the War of Independence, 1919–1921, was obtained from this wonderful source.

The Irish National Archive, Bishop Street, Dublin 2, for the file relating to Sam Maguire's dismissal from the Irish Post Office.

Mr Barry Attoe and Ms Ashley March of the British Postal Museum & Archive, London, who provided details of Sam Maguire's employment in the British Post Office.

Mr Mark Gottsche, treasurer, London GAA and Mr Pat Griffin, author of *Gaelic Hearts: A History of London GAA, 1896–1996,* for information about Sam Maguire's playing career with London Hibernians and the evolution of the GAA in London.

Mr Oliver Frawley for assistance with research in London.

Local historian Tim Reen, Rathbarry, County Cork, for information about Sam Maguire's attendance at the local 'University of the Mountain', and the Reerasta-Ardagh Historical Society for information about the discovery of the Ardagh Chalice.

Mr George Maguire, Reenascreena, Rosscarbery, County Cork, for the cover photograph of the Sam Maguire statue.

Mr Davy Walsh and Ms Betty Walsh, Ferrybank, Waterford, for information about the Waterford Crystal replica of the Sam Maguire Cup presented to the winning All-Ireland captains on the 75th anniversary of the first presentation of the cup.

To my brothers-in-law Michael O'Donovan, Ballinacarriga, County Cork, and Jerome O'Donovan, Ballincollig, County Cork, for their help, and to Mr Finny O'Donovan of Ballinacarriga, County Cork, for reading the text.

The Dunmanway Historical Society museum, Main Street, Dunmanway, County Cork, for access to its file on Sam Maguire.

Finally to my brother James Connolly, Dunmanway, who was my agent in Dunmanway and who was always available to help.

FOREWORD

Táim breá sásta an deis seo a bheith agam fáilte a chur roimh an foilseachán seo agus scéal Sam Mhic Uidhir a chur i láthair in aon leabhar amháin mar atá anseo.

Irish society confers special status on those who become known by one name and one name only. 'Micko', 'Paidí' and 'Micheál' are just three from the GAA stable of greats that spring to mind, referencing legends of our games who enthralled, entertained and fascinated across generations for so many years – and continue to do so. It is not recognition that can be claimed or sought; it is conferred and earned, and is the clearest indication of being held in high regard by a cross-section of society at a given point in time.

Alongside them – both literally and metaphorically – is of course 'Sam'. While usage of the three-lettered byword for 'Buan Chorn Sam Maguire', to give it its full title, is informal and casual, behind the instant recognition lies respect for one of the most recognisable artefacts in Irish life.

The ornate silver cup based on the Ardagh Chalice is the most coveted trophy in Irish sport, underlining the appeal and reach of football across this island and further still. Its shining glint never fails to command attention, turning heads everywhere it goes, provoking interest and curiosity, and embellishing every occasion it graces. To those enmeshed in the games it also alludes to the history that underpins the GAA and the storied layers on which our foundations are built.

Isn't it somewhat ironic that the two most recognisable trophies in the GAA – the Sam Maguire and Liam Mac-Carthy Cups – are named after men who served the GAA so well not in Ireland, but in London? Yet in many ways things have come full circle, with our international network blossoming and the links with home through our games stronger than ever before.

I congratulate all who were involved with this project in bringing together the story of the man behind the cup. I sincerely hope that it will provide many of our members and followers with food for thought the next time his name is uttered in the context of the great game that is Gaelic football.

Rath Dé ar an obair,
Aogán Ó Fearghail,
Uachtarán Chumann Lúthchleas Gael

INTRODUCTION

Sam Maguire's life began as Ireland commenced the final fight for independence. The period from 1877 to 1927 was one of constant struggle in Ireland and included the agitation for Home Rule, the 1916 Rising, the War of Independence (1919–1921) and the Civil War (1922–1923). Maguire would play a major role in Ireland's fight for independence, taking a senior role in the Irish Republican Army (IRA) in London, as well as playing an important part in encouraging the development of the Gaelic Athletic Association (GAA). Yet Maguire himself remains a little-known figure, remembered largely because his name was given to the cup that is presented each year to the team that wins the All-Ireland football championship final.

I have chosen to write this book in two parts – one looks at the story of Maguire himself, the other at the cup through which he is remembered. Sadly, during his lifetime Maguire seems to have been content to work in the background and not seek recognition. He left no personal records, such as diaries or letters, to describe his role in the War of Independence in London. Although this was true of the majority of participants, many of them later gave detailed statements to the Bureau of Military History (BMH), a process that did not begin until twenty years after Maguire's death. Luckily, he impressed many of those with whom he worked during those years and they recalled his activities in their statements. It is, therefore, possible to describe his role in the IRA to some extent.

His friends and comrades in the IRA clearly thought a great deal of him as they decided to dedicate a cup in his name. So I could think of no better way to commemorate the man than to conclude this book with a look at the creation of the Sam Maguire Cup and some of the significant finals where it has been awarded, as well as providing a miscellany of interesting facts about the finals since the cup was first awarded in 1928.

This is the story of the man and the cup.

1

DUNMANWAY YOUTH

The All-Ireland Senior Football Championship final is attended by a capacity crowd and is usually one of the most-viewed programmes on Irish television. The captain of the winning team is presented with the Sam Maguire Cup.

On the second Sunday of September each year in Dunmanway, County Cork, a ceremony takes place at St Mary's Church of Ireland, where Sam Maguire is buried. Members of the local GAA club, the Dohenys, attend the Sunday service. Following the service, the congregation gathers at Maguire's grave in the churchyard to lay a wreath. In 2015 the chairperson of the Cork County Board of the GAA attended the ceremony and brought with him the Sam Maguire Cup. To quote a phrase often used by the captain of the winning county's team, 'Sam came home.'

Dunmanway, approximately sixty kilometres west of Cork city, was the terminus of the railway from the city to the south-west in 1877, the year Maguire was born. Three trains ran to Cork every weekday and one on Sunday. Travel beyond Dunmanway had to be made by coach and mail car. Another important feature of the town was that the local post office contained a telegraph office. The railway and telegraph have recently been labelled the 'nineteenth-century internet'; they meant that Dunmanway was connected to the larger world.

Dunmanway's commercial directory of 1871 listed a very diverse variety and large number of shops and tradesmen, three hotels – including a Royal Hotel – and a pawnbroker. Dunmanway also had a Catholic chapel, an Anglican church and a Methodist church. The district had six Royal Irish Constabulary (RIC) stations and thirteen schools. There were three local papers: *The Cork Examiner*, *The Skibbereen Eagle* (which was famous for its line 'keep an eye on Russia' in the late nineteenth century) and *The Southern Star* (which would eventually take over and shut down the *Eagle*).

Sam Maguire was born to John and Jane Maguire in the townland of Mallabracka, six-and-a-half kilometres north of Dunmanway, on 11 March 1877.[1] He was one of seven children: William (or Willie) was the eldest, then Mary (Moll or Molly), John (Jack), Richard (Dick), Paul, Sam and Elizabeth. The family were members of the Church of Ireland, which in 1871 represented about twelve per cent of the population of Dunmanway. Although in the past it has been suggested that the surname Maguire was unusual in Cork, the 1911 census for Cork contains at least a hundred families with this surname, spread all over Cork city and county, from Ballycotton in the east to Castletownbere in the west.

The Maguires farmed 200 acres as tenants of Robert Ellis. The land was part of the Shouldham estate, which in the 1870s amounted to over 13,000 acres. The Shouldham family had originated in Norfolk. In the early eighteenth century Edmond Shouldham of Ardtully, County Kerry, married Mary MacCarthy, daughter and heiress of MacCarthy Spaniagh of Dunmanway. However, the land worked by the Maguires had only about 50–60 acres of good farmland.

As was common practice at the time, Willie, as the eldest son, inherited the farm. He served in the Church of Ireland in Dunmanway as a vestryman on the committee elected by the members of the parish to run its affairs. Willie never married, and neither did Mary nor Elizabeth, who both remained at home. Sam, along with two of his other brothers, Jack and Dick, went to work in the post office in London. Their brother Paul married a Catholic and, perhaps because of local disapproval of the mixed marriage, decided to emigrate to the USA. Despite the large number of children in the Maguire family, there are no direct descendants.

The year Sam Maguire was born was the end of a nineteenth-century economic bubble. This was a food bubble rather than a property bubble: in the thirty years between the worst year of the Great Famine or An Gorta Mór – 1847, known as 'Black '47' – and the year of Maguire's birth food prices rose very rapidly, as did the incomes of Irish farmers. The year 1877 in Ireland was the nineteenth-century equivalent of 2007, when the economy moved to a plateau of prosperity before collapsing into a severe economic downturn. The later years of the decade brought a devastating combination of very poor weather, harvest failure for three years in succession and international economic depression. The bad weather meant that the harvests were the worst since the Famine and potato blight followed. This led to what became known as the Mini-Famine or An Gorta Beag.

At the time of Maguire's birth, the main development in farming was a switch from tillage to cattle, caused by a fall in cereal prices and a rise in cattle prices. Another reason was that tillage was more labour intensive and there was a post-Great Famine decline in the number of agricultural labourers. The shorthorn was the dominant breed of cattle; it was divided into the dairy breed and the slightly larger beef breed. It is more than likely that the Maguires would have had the dairy breed, because it was a dual-purpose animal that could both produce milk and be sold as beef. It was regarded as ideal for the Irish climate and very suitable for low-input farming systems such as those that existed in Ireland in this period.

The milk from these cows was mainly used to make butter to sell. The Maguires' butter would have been sold to dealers at the market held on Tuesdays in Dunmanway, and also probably sent to the Cork Butter Exchange, which at this time was regarded as the main provider of butter in Ireland and Britain, exporting butter to many countries. As incomes rose in England, so did the demand for beef, and the cattle would also have been sold for this purpose. In addition to beef, the carcass yielded cheaper cuts, such as the liver and kidneys, and the fat could be used to make lard or dripping.

The essential link between Irish farmers like the Maguires and the English market was the cattle dealer. Cattle were ready for the market at the end of the summer and sold at the fair in Dunmanway. They were then transported by train from the local station, a practice that continued until late in the twentieth century, as long as the fairs were held in Dunmanway. Some animals would require further fattening, which would be done on land owned by the dealers. To avoid a glut of cattle arriving on the English market, they would gradually release the animals to the market. The dealers had very good connections with the buyers in England and a very sophisticated system existed, connecting dealers, bankers, shipping companies and English buyers.

The Maguires, like most people living on farms at this time, would also have grown most of their own food, such as potatoes, drunk milk from the family's cows and collected eggs from the poultry. Bread was mostly homemade, as was butter. Bread could also be bought from the local shops in Dunmanway; it was known as 'shop bread' and was regarded as a luxury or treat for the youngsters. By the time of Sam Maguire's birth, tea – initially a drink of the upper classes – had become very common and would have been part of his daily diet.

In farmhouses, typically only the kitchen would have a fire, so it was the centre of daily life. The fire was an open hearth with a movable metal bar known as a 'crane', which hung over the open fire. The pots had hooks that hung from the crane as food was cooked. This required a delicate balance: too close to the fire and the food would burn, too far away and it would not cook properly.

People would have risen and gone to bed at times dictated by the season. In the summer, this meant up at cockcrow, literally, and late to bed. In the winter less work was required on the farm, so rising was later, but the dark nights also meant early to bed. Children were expected to help out on the farm with tasks such as churning butter, milking cows and saving the hay. The latter was crucial, as it provided feed for the cattle during the winter. At night there would be occasional visits from neighbours or visits to neighbours. Some houses in the locality would be known as 'rambling houses', in which gatherings took place on a regular basis. In West Cork this is known as 'screarting' (an English word derived from the Irish word scoraíocht).

There were no organised sports at this time. Young people in Maguire's locality swam in the local pool near their home, known as 'the falls'. They would have engaged in road bowling and might have played some primitive form of football with a ball made from an animal bladder. It is evident from the sources that there was also a 'tradition of running, jumping and weight throwing'.[2] Maguire's social network would have been limited to schoolfriends and the children of neighbouring farms.

Maguire's education began in the Model School in Dunmanway, which opened on 13 August 1849. The first Model School had been opened in Upper Merrion Street, Dublin, on 10 February 1834, three years after the establishment of the national system of primary education in Ireland. This institution, better known as the Central Model School, was later at the heart of a larger system of provincial schools – District Model Schools – which were established from 1849 across the country. The Dunmanway school leased a farm of eleven-and-a-half acres, later increased to forty-three acres, because it initially provided an agricultural education for boys.

The youngest children, referred to as 'infants', were taught the '3Rs' – reading, writing and arithmetic. As the children grew older, they also learned geography and bookkeeping. In addition, the older boys learned science, horticulture and agriculture. The language used in teaching in all the Model Schools was English; even in areas where Irish was spoken, it was not taught. The school was divided into a junior section that provided the standard six years of primary education, and a senior section consisting of a seventh year. Maguire attended both junior and senior departments, learning subjects such as algebra, mensuration (the study of geometric magnitudes), geometry, agriculture, line drawing and music.

When he finished in the Model School, Maguire attended a school run by Michael Madden in Ardfield, a few miles from Clonakilty.[3] While a pupil there, he lived with his uncle, an employee at Castlefreke, the home of Lord Carbery. Michael Madden (appointed as a national teacher in May 1868), known as Master Madden, ran the boys' school and his wife, Sarah (appointed in October 1868), the girls'. They specialised in preparing pupils for the post office and the British civil-service examinations.

Before the middle of the nineteenth century, there was no formal method of recruitment to the post office or the civil service. It was based on 'who you know, not what you know'; family and political connections decided who should be recruited, which led to a very poor quality of recruit. Anthony

Trollope described the hopelessly unprofessional way he was hired by the post office in 1834:

> I was asked to copy some lines from the *Times* newspaper with an old quill pen, and at once made a series of blots and false spellings ... (The next day) I was seated at a desk without any further reference to my competency.[4]

As the British Empire expanded and became difficult to administer due to the complex nature of the work and the poor quality of the civil service, it was recognised that the quality of recruits had to be improved. Sir Stafford Northcote, the legal secretary to the Board of Trade and later a Conservative party MP and leader, and Sir Charles Trevelyan, the assistant secretary to the Treasury from 1840 to 1859, proposed a change in 1853. Trevelyan (the one mentioned in the song 'The Fields of Athenry') was horrified by the poor quality of men in the civil service. He once described a colleague as 'a gentleman who really could neither read nor write, he was almost an idiot'. Trevelyan has also been described as 'a total stickler, intolerant of all fripperies. He liked to correct his Treasury colleagues' punctuation and was always keen on saving money on candles and newspapers. And he had no small talk.' His brother-in-law Lord Macaulay, the famous British historian, said of him, 'His topics, even in courtship, are steam navigation, the education of the natives, the equalisation of the sugar duties, and the substitution of the Roman for the Arabic alphabet in Oriental languages.'[5]

The proposed improvements meant adopting a formal method of recruitment, based on competitive examinations. But there was resistance, and when the report was released, 'jaws dropped in the gentlemen's clubs of Piccadilly. Queen Victoria wrote to Gladstone, worried that it would let the wrong sort of person in. The Prime Minister, Lord John Russell, was outraged too: "In future our board of examiners will be in place of the Queen, our institutions will become as harshly republican as possible. I cannot say how seriously I feel all this," he wrote. From the press came their worst possible insult, then as now – it was too European. Too German, even.'[6]

Queen Victoria, it seemed, was right to be worried, because this method of recruitment meant that young Irishmen who held nationalist views, such as Sam Maguire and Michael Collins, could apply for and be appointed to positions in the UK post office and civil service. R. F. Foster, in *Vivid Faces*, his history describing the leading personalities of the revolutionary period, says of the volunteers who returned from London to fight in 1916:

They too had been radicalised through Gaelic League circles in London. Ó Brian's list [of these volunteers] sketches the kind of networks which stretched from the remote south-west of Ireland to the Irish-Irelander circles of Edwardian London, via the imperial structure of the Royal Mail, creating an unexpected but recognisable pattern of radicalisation.[7]

In nineteenth-century Ireland there was very little work available for those without land of their own. The system of inheritance in post-Famine Ireland was such that the land was not divided between the children in a family, but was inherited by the eldest son as a complete unit. Daughters would be expected to marry; in the case of substantial farmers they would be provided with a dowry to attract a husband. Younger sons were required to find off-farm employment. However, the switch from tillage to cattle following the Great Famine reduced the demand for labour, while consolidation of farms into larger holdings also meant dislocation of rural labourers. The few jobs available were poorly paid. Because there was little future in Ireland for these people, emigration became more attractive.

The change in the system of recruitment to the UK post office and civil service created attractive, permanent, pensionable employment for these people. This was the nineteenth-century equivalent of the introduction of free education in Ireland in the 1960s, which opened up third-level education to a much wider cohort of students. Maguire was fortunate to be able to take advantage of the changes.

Michael Madden's school was very successful in training pupils for entry to the post office and became known as the 'university of the mountain', as it was situated in the townland of Mountain Common. (People from Ardfield were referred to as being from The Mountain.) At the time, schools were inspected by department inspectors who awarded a prize for the 'best school' in the country, known as the 'Carlisle and Blake Premium'. Ardfield won the prize nine times, and following its last win Madden decided to withdraw from the competition to give other schools a chance of winning. Apparently the school was so successful 'that when a male child was born … the neighbours would say "Musha, God bless him. It's the fine [postal] sorter he'll make."'[8]

Of much more significance for Maguire's life was the fact that Michael Madden was a dedicated nationalist. Both Madden and his father were reputed to have been involved in several attempted revolts against British rule in the nineteenth century. It could be assumed that Madden was, in the language of the day, an advanced nationalist who would support the concept of an armed struggle to achieve Irish independence. Because Madden had very strong nationalist views, it is reasonable to assume that he imparted this perspective to his pupils. The standard curriculum in the state schools did not include Irish history, but Madden taught this in his school. He also had a field beside the school where, following the foundation of the GAA in 1884, the pupils played Gaelic games.

Given the fact that 'all things Irish' and Gaelic football would not have been part of Maguire's education in the Model School, or his Protestant family's cultural and political outlook, it is logical to conclude that his time in Ardfield school had a most important effect on his later career in the GAA and the Irish Republican Brotherhood (IRB). Maguire's brothers Jack and Dick also went to the school. Another pupil was J. J. Walsh of Bandon; Walsh was Minister for Posts and Telegraphs in the Irish Free State when he secured a job in the Irish post office for Maguire on his return from England in 1923.

All three of the Maguire brothers who attended Madden's school went to London to work for the post office. It was easy for them to travel by train to Cork and then on to London. The British Postal Museum & Archive records state that Samuel Maguire was appointed as a sorter in November 1897 in the London central office.[9] He was twenty years of age when he started this work.

According to P. S. O'Hegarty (member of the IRB central council, author of several histories of the period, and secretary of the Department of Posts and Telegraphs from 1922 to 1945):

I had no experience of the working conditions in these [sorting] offices, but I gathered that they were hard and sometimes difficult in that a number of the supervising officers were anti-Irish, and made things as difficult as possible for the Irish boys. But Mount Pleasant was never referred to other than as Mount Misery, and I gathered that, outside that, the conditions in the other offices were tolerable enough.[10]

O'Hegarty goes on to state that he had a very good experience in his own work in the civil service.

2

THE IRISH AND THE GAA IN ENGLAND

During the Great Famine (1845–1849), approximately a million people left Ireland. For many, England was the destination of choice. The men who went to London worked as unskilled labourers, while the women found jobs as domestic servants or in the clothing industry. The low social status of the Irish and the disorienting impact of the move from rural Ireland to a huge city meant that the Irish community was demoralised and lacking in confidence. The reaction of many Irish emigrants was to discard any remaining element of Irish identity, but others did attempt to retain this heritage. Initially the Catholic Church was very important in this effort, but politics quickly began to take an increasingly prominent role in the promotion of an Irish nationalist awakening.

The emergence of prominent politicians such as Charles Stewart Parnell – leader of the Irish Parliamentary Party in the British House of Commons – and the agitation for Home Rule in Ireland meant that by the 1870s the political awareness of the Irish in London had developed to a high level. As Stephen Moore and Paul Darby explain:

> The promotion of nationalist politics amongst the diaspora was crucial in terms of the development of a distinctive Irish ethnicity in Britain. The desire of the majority of Irish migrants to see the constitutional relationship between Ireland and Britain redefined not only fed into the divide between Irish immigrants and the host society, it was also key in helping the émigrés develop the political consciousness in which elements of their ethnicity were rooted. The emergence of a well organised, coordinated and popular Irish nationalist movement in the second half of the nineteenth century in Ireland was clearly important in the political mobilisation of the Irish in Britain.[1]

This change in political consciousness was accompanied by an increased awareness of Irish culture, with the 'Gaelic Revival' epitomised by organisations such as the Gaelic League. As Moore and Darby indicate: 'By the end of the nineteenth century, the Irish diaspora in Britain had gradually become a settled, ethnically distinct community, numbering almost one million among a population of thirty million.'[2] However, they also note that while the Irish community in England was well served by cultural organisations, the same was not true of sporting organisations.

In the nineteenth century Ireland was part of the United Kingdom and, because of this, was heavily influenced by developments in England, particularly the attitude to sport. 'Cruel sports' such as bull-baiting and cock-fighting were outlawed in the mid 1830s. Sport came to be seen as very important for the development of young men – 'a healthy mind in a healthy body'. It was suggested that playing a rule-based sport would develop a strong character in a man, who would learn to be gracious in victory and in defeat.

In November 1884 Michael Cusack, Maurice Davin and others founded the GAA in Thurles. In England Parnell's Irish National League, a nationalist political party founded in October 1882 and controlled by Parnell to support the fight for Home Rule for Ireland, attempted to create its own sporting association independent of the GAA in Ireland. The League was strong in London and was the main organising force for Gaelic games in the city. It regarded Gaelic games as an important means of creating a cultural and political consciousness amongst the Irish in England. Moreover, as members of parliament (MPs) did not receive a salary because it was assumed that they would be 'gentlemen of independent means' who had no need of one, some Irish MPs saw the possibility of using Gaelic games as a fundraiser. However, other nationalists, including the members of the IRB, the secretive revolutionary movement that sought an independent Irish republic by any means and had a significant influence on the GAA in Ireland, thought that any Gaelic sporting organisation would be stronger if it were linked to the GAA, and so the GAA opposed the Irish National League's plans.

In 1895 two clubs linked with the Irish National League were formed in London – the Milesians and Robert Emmets. At the same time two non-Irish National League clubs, the Hibernian Athletic club and the Exiles of Erin were established. The majority of the members of the Hibernian club were postal workers. In an effort to boost the non-Irish National League clubs, the GAA sent two hurling teams, Munster and Leinster, to play an exhibition game and an all-Ireland football team to play a London selection. The hurling teams marched in a procession to advertise the games, and the following day, Easter Monday 1896, the matches were held in the Stamford Bridge stadium. The event was a great success and prompted the clubs affiliated with the Irish National League to change over to the GAA.

On 10 June 1896 a meeting was held to form a county board. In order to do this it was necessary to have at least five teams. In London these teams were: Hibernians (North London), Exiles of Erin (South London), Sons of Erin (East London), Fulham O'Connells (West London) and a team called Brothers Sheares. Interestingly, the last of these was not heard of again after its initial listing for the board and, in a letter to a local paper, the secretary of the board did not mention any delegates from this club.[3]

Liam MacCarthy (for whom the All-Ireland hurling cup is named) was appointed as the board's secretary. MacCarthy was born in England and became a highly successful businessman running a packaging firm. He was very prominent in promoting the GAA, and his first period as chairman of the London County Board ran from 1898 to 1907.

The GAA central council meeting in Thurles on 9 November that year welcomed 'the establishment of … the South London Athletic Club and the Islington Hibernians Athletic Club' and warned that the council 'would not recognise any clubs … run under political auspices'.[4] The latter was, of course, directed at the Irish National League.

Liam MacCarthy and other prominent members of the London board were members of the IRB and saw the GAA as an important source of recruits for the organisation in both Ireland and England. The growth of the GAA in England was not as rapid as in Ireland, but it did grow. MacCarthy spoke frequently of the difficulties facing the organisation in England due to continued anti-Irish prejudice. This prejudice was probably fed by the Home Rule agitation and also Irish support for the Boers fighting the British Army during the second Boer War (1899–1902). The hostility was apparent in the difficulty the GAA had in obtaining access to grounds controlled by local authorities.

At the GAA annual congress on 21 September 1901 a motion was submitted that 'England be considered as a Province of Ireland for the purposes of the Gaelic Athletic Association'; the motion passed. Its stated purpose was that 'the teams in England could form a Provincial Council and take part in the inter-provincial championships'.[5]

London tabled a motion for the 1911 GAA convention that rule thirteen of the official guide 'Containing the Constitution and Rules of the G.A.A. ... published by authority of the Central Council [of the GAA]' – the ban on GAA members playing foreign games – would not apply in London.[6] At the time, clubs in London all discussed and voted on the issue. The results were as follows: Rooneys – unanimously against the motion; Geraldines (the club to which Michael Collins belonged) – unanimously against the motion; Hibernians (the club to which Sam Maguire belonged) – declared that the motion was illegal and club delegates should vote against it; Brian Boru – majority of two in favour of the motion; Cusacks – majority of two in favour of the motion; Milesians – undecided, club delegates given a free hand.

Despite such significant opposition, the motion was

passed by twenty-five votes to twenty, because four of the Hibernian delegates disobeyed the club's instructions and voted for it. The motion received only four out of seventy votes at the GAA congress. While the motion was accepted by London, it had no chance of being passed by the GAA convention in Ireland. The split in the London GAA over the issue led to those who favoured the ban laying plans to create a new county board.

After the dispute was over, the Hibernian delegates who voted for the motion, broke from their old club and formed a new one called Young Ireland. At the first county board meeting after the congress, the Rooneys club proposed that this Young Ireland club should be suspended – they claimed it was a club created to break the rule and the suspension should last until all its members complied with rule thirteen. The motion was defeated. Following this, the Rooneys, Geraldines and 'Hibernians, with the newly formed Thomas Davis club, created a new county board, with Sam Maguire as president. Under the new county board, both Maguire and Michael Collins acted as football referees.

Maguire was elected as treasurer of the Hibernian Club in July 1901 and re-elected to that post in 1902. He served alongside Liam MacCarthy as vice-president from 1902 until 1906 and was an active player during this period. He held the position of president in 1907 and again in 1908. He stepped down in 1909, but returned to the position in 1912, serving until 1915.

3

SAM MAGUIRE'S PARTICIPATION IN ALL-IRELAND FINALS

Sam Maguire did not play football for the local Dunmanway club, the Dohenys, before he went to work in the post office in London in 1897 as the GAA was considered to be a nationalist, primarily Catholic organisation. It would not have been regarded as an organisation that Protestant men and boys would join.

In 1901, following the acceptance of England as a province for the purposes of the GAA, a new All-Ireland format was introduced. The four provincial championships would be played as usual. They played in the 'Home' championship, with the winners of the 'Home' final going on to face the London champions in the 'Away' All-Ireland final. The purpose of the change was to assist the development of the GAA in London. As Eoghan Corry explains, 'Britain had been declared a province of Ireland at the previous congress with an irony befitting the nationalist GAA and that meant London Irish got a bye in to the All-Ireland for the first time.'[1]

Often All-Ireland finals would not be played in the calendar year of the championship, but rather in the following year or even later. For example, the 1900 'Away' final was played in 1902. It was not until 1909 that the scheduled games were actually played within the designated year of the national championships.

It was the practice until 1923 that the club champions would represent their county in the All-Ireland competition. Maguire's club, London Hibernians, were champions for many of the early years of the London GAA between 1897 and 1910, and several times during the time when Maguire was a player – thus they played in several 'Away' All-Ireland finals. Interestingly, the club that won the county championship was allowed to pick players from all the clubs in the county. For example, the first London team to take part in the All-Ireland final was made up of players from five clubs, while their opponents, Tipperary, used players from six clubs.

Between 1896 and 1913, the number of players on a team was seventeen – the teams on which Maguire played consisted of this number. Corry states that this 'caused a continuous scrimmage that moved backwards and forwards along the field. Blake [a GAA secretary] felt that the formation should be broken into clear lines with more space for players to move.'[2]

The large number of players meant that Gaelic football was not a very attractive spectator sport. At the 1913 GAA convention a motion proposed by Harry Boland (a senior member of the IRB and good friend of Michael Collins) to reduce the number of men to fifteen was passed. The first inter-county game with fifteen players on each team was the Croke Memorial Cup final between Louth and Kerry in May 1913. This was a competition held to raise funds to erect a monument to Archbishop Croke, the first patron of the GAA, after whom the stadium in Jones' Road, Dublin, was later named.

In the early days of Gaelic football, the goal was a soccer-style goal. The only way to score at that time was by a goal (putting the ball through the goal mouth). Many games ended without a goal being scored, another thing which made this an unappealing game for spectators. To overcome this difficulty, 'point' posts were introduced – two posts stood twenty-one yards either side of the goals. A point was scored by putting the ball between these posts.

Maguire played his first final in the 1900 All-Ireland football 'Away' final on 26 October 1902 and is recorded as one of London's two scorers. His brother Jack was also a member of the London team. The football and hurling matches were played on the same day; both were played between London and Tipperary teams. The participation of the London team led to some excessive sentiment being expressed by journalists. One reporter wrote that it proved that the 'Gaelic heart could resist the corrosive influences of a foreign environment' such as England.[3]

The Freeman's Journal reported that 'the Hibernians arrived at the North Wall in Dublin at 2.00 a.m. and "put up" at the North Star Hotel'.[4] The Tipperary champions, Clonmel Shamrocks, were scheduled to travel from Clonmel to arrive at Dublin's Kingsbridge station (now Heuston) in time for the game. However, the Tipperary champions were an hour late and it was 2.10 p.m. before the first match began. The newspaper report continued:

> This was the only hitch which occurred in the whole proceedings, but it will, of course, be observed that the Central Council were in no way to blame in connection with the matter, though it must be stated the delay of the special train caused considerable disappointment to those of our business men who had to return to their concerns before 2 o'clock without witnessing the matches.
>
> Order was well maintained throughout the play, and at no time did an incursion of the grounds take place. It is, however,

quite true that spectators found their way inside the railings, but that was because there was not sufficient room for them outside. The throng of spectators was never so great at Jones's road, but great as it was it was orderly and, when the time came, enthusiastic even to the verge of excitement.[5]

A match report in *The Cork Examiner* stated that 'the Tipperary men were again successful … The match was somewhat fast and strong play prevailed at times, but the referee was strict and did not allow to it go beyond the bounds.'[6] Mr T. H. Redmond refereed the football match. Clonmel Shamrocks won by 14 points: Clonmel 3–07, London Hibernians 0–02. As a postscript to this story, Pat Griffin notes:

> The game signalled the end of the Clonmel Shamrocks. They had waited until the London party were on the high seas before demanding extra expenses. They were eventually suspended and the dispute ended up in the law courts where the GAA were admonished for their actions.[7]

The London Hibernians competed again in the 1901 final, when the opposition was Dublin's Isles of the Sea (which no longer exists as a club). Once again, London suffered a heavy defeat when the final was played on 2 August 1903. The newspaper report is very brief. *The Cork Examiner* stated:

'Mr McCarthy also refereed this match, in which, however, very little interest was taken. From the start it was apparent that Isles of the Sea were much superior to their fellow countrymen from across Channel.'[8] The score was Isles of the Sea 0–14 and Hibernians 0–02, although the Hibernians' performance was apparently better than that in the game against Clonmel Shamrocks.

As a sign of the increasing strength and popularity of the GAA, there was a dinner after the final played in 1903 in the Mansion House, hosted by the lord mayor. Liam MacCarthy responded to the toast 'Ireland a nation' by saying that 'it meant their people staying at home and plenty of work for them'. He also said that the victory of the London team in the All-Ireland Hurling final for 1901, played on the same day as the football final:

> ... had roused the passion and spirit of the diners and Dan O'Callaghan's speech celebrated the achievements of Irish exiles. The opening words of his speech give a flavour of his contribution:
>
> 'Have we not given an O'Donnell, Duke of Tetuan to Spain, a Taafe [prime minister and friend of the emperor] to Austria, a queen to Sweden [Queen Brigida Haraldsdotter] and the predecessor of [President] Roosevelt, the martyred [President] McKinley had in his veins the blood of an Antrim rebel ...'[9]

The 1902 'Away' final was played on 11 September 1904 in the Athletic Grounds in Cork to mark the opening of the ground. The London team travelled by boat to Dublin and by train to Cork. They had breakfast in the North Star Hotel before catching the train. The lord mayor of Cork officially opened the ground. The opposition was Bray Emmets, representing Dublin. The score was 2–08 to 0–04 in favour of Bray Emmets. According to *The Universe* of 17 September, Maguire was one of London's best players. A newspaper report said of the game, 'the sympathies of the crowd were with them [Hibernians] for the Dublin football tactics, too redolent of soccer and rugby, are distasteful to a really Gaelic audience'.[10]

That year the London players refused to attend the dinner hosted by the lord mayor, because he was alleged to have contributed to a monument to British soldiers who died in the Boer War. Another offence was that he was due to open a rugby ground for Cork Constitution. The team also objected to the fact that soldiers in uniform were admitted to the Athletic Grounds for the match.

In 1896, to celebrate the silver jubilee of his appointment as a bishop, Archbishop Croke had donated two silver cups to the GAA:

The Croke Cup quickly became the GAA's second most prestigious competition … organised on a knockout basis parallel to the All-Ireland championship but caused so much fixture congestion that after victories by the Dublin footballers in 1896 and the Wexford footballers in 1897 the trophies were awarded to the All-Ireland champions.[11]

In 1904 the competition for the football cup was revived and in the London was invited to play for the Croke Cup rather than for the All-Ireland title that year. From 1909 to 1916 the cup was used for a competition between the losing provincial finalists. In 1916 that competition ended and the cup was retired. After 1926 the cups were awarded to the winners of the National League finals 'before ending up in the GAA museum in Croke Park'.[12]

Maguire's last All-Ireland final was played in 1905, on 12 November, for the 1903 All-Ireland. London Hibernians played the Kerry champions, Tralee Mitchels. Given their strong performance earlier in the year in the Croke Cup, London's expectations were high. Griffin explains that 'Captain Sam Maguire had gained unstinted praise for the team he had selected. He had strengthened the forward division which was a let-down in the Croke Cup final.'[13] However, the Tralee Mitchels were already leading the game at half-time by 0–08 to 0–00. Although London played with the wind and did better in the second half, the final score was 0–11 to 0–03. This final was the first of Kerry's many All-Ireland victories.

Liam MacCarthy, the London County Board chairman at the time, said of this final:

> I am satisfied lack of combination told against us. At any rate we would want to learn a new set of rules every time we come to Ireland. In my opinion they seem too elastic. One time it's keep to the ball and dribble it; at another a game of leap-frog would not be out of place.[14]

London GAA member and prominent nationalist P. S. O'Hegarty suggested that the journey on the deck of the boat to North Wall in winter was 'not conducive to athletics'. He also alleged that the Kerry players were very clever in the way that they obtained frees (a 'free' being a free kick awarded to a team when the opposing team commits a breach of the rules, or foul): 'When a Kerry man fielded a ball, and had not kicking room, he immediately turned his back on his opponent, who naturally put his arms around his opponent to punch the ball out of his grasp.'[15]

In contrast, the *Kerry Sentinel* reported on 15 November:

> ... on different occasions during the game the play was of a particularly rough character and several of the Kerry players had to retire from the field, some of them very badly hurt owing to the tactics of those on the opposing side. However,

despite every effort on the part of the Londoners, they had to taste the bitter fruits of defeat, and the Kerry men proved conclusively that they were by long odds the better men.

The field arrangements too could have been better, as during the last half of the match the spectators crossed the barriers and encroached to a considerable extent on the field.

Immediately on the start Kerry broke away and scored, and from this to the end of the half hour had the ball practically at their mercy, and went over to the second half with 8 points to their credit against London-Irish nil.

The London Irish scored three points which left the play at call of time – Kerry, 11 points, London-Irish, 3 points.[16]

By the 1905 All-Ireland championship, the format of the finals seems to have changed, although there is no record of what prompted this change in the minutes of the central council. London were in the quarter-final of that championship, played on Sunday 5 August 1906, and Milesians were representing London. Even though Maguire's club were not the London champions that year and did not qualify for the finals, as noted previously the winning team could select players from other clubs to play in the All-Ireland and Maguire was one of those so chosen. The *Irish Independent* reported on Monday 6 August that 'there was a fairish crowd … From a weak kick-out London were nearly in difficulties but playing against the wind Sam Maguire out-manoeuvred

McCann and amidst great cheering the Exiles scored a magnificent goal … the ball was rushed down the field, and Sam Maguire again did the needful for Clan London.'

At the end of the first half, London led by 1–03 to 0–04. Maguire scored 1–01. Unfortunately, the lack of training by the London team became evident in the second half, as at one point three London players were down 'winded' at the same time, and Dublin took the game. P. S. O'Hegarty wrote in his monthly column in *Inis Fáil* that in the first twenty minutes:

> London were all over the Dublin men; they fielded well, kicked remarkably well, and, though the marking was only indifferent they almost neutralised this fault by jumping for the ball which they got in most cases. But after that period, they seemed to fall away … overall the match was a fine one to look at, fast and vigorous. The spectators considered it the best display London has yet given, but the method of picking the team will have to be radically altered … if Sam Maguire and Paddy Sheehan were not fit for their respective proper places as back and left scoring it was obviously unfair both to them and to the other men to pick them for places where they are not accustomed to play … it is a common fallacy that all places are alike on a Gaelic team but that does not work in practice.[17]

The last time London played in an All-Ireland final was the 1908 final, played on 3 October 1909. Dublin beat them with a score of 1–10 to 0–04. This final had the smallest audience for any All-Ireland final. Following the very poor performance of the London team, it was decided to end the 'Away' final for good.

On the day after the 1906 All-Ireland semi-final – played on 4 August 1907 – London took on the Bray Emmets in Richard (Boss) Croker's ground in Sandyford. Croker was born in Clonakilty, County Cork, in 1841, and his family emigrated to New York city in 1846. He was born a Protestant, but he converted to Catholicism on his first marriage.

In 1886 Croker took control of the Tammany Hall organisation, which ran the Democratic Party in New York. The party relied on the votes of Irish and German immigrants. The organisation claimed to be able to fill every city post in New York, from mayor to porter. The employees would pay a percentage of their wages to the organisation, which also took protection money from gamblers and prostitutes. During Croker's time in control, Tammany Hall was said to have had 90,000 members.

Croker did not make his money directly from the organisation. Instead, he established a real-estate partnership and sold land to the city of New York. He used inside information about proposed developments to buy up land at low prices and sell it at a premium to the city. He also made money from contracts awarded by New York to firms he controlled. In reply to a question from an investigation commission about whether he was working for his own pocket, he replied 'All the time, same as you.'[18] His reign in New York ended when revelations of corruption led to the loss of office by Tammany representatives in 1901.

Croker returned to Ireland and built a mansion named 'Glencairn' in Sandyford, Dublin, on fifty-one acres. He spent £75,000 (more than £6,000,000 in today's money) on the house. Recognising that the area was one likely to be developed, he bought an additional 500 acres and built stables and a miniature racecourse on the land. In 1906 he offered to supply a one-off cup for a Gaelic football match.

The proceeds of the match, played in 1907, went to the Catholic church at Glencullen. Despite their loss to Dublin on the previous day, the London team won on a scoreline of 2–05 to 0–07. Liam MacCarthy accepted the cup for London. He said that while they were taking back the Boss Croker Cup, they would not rest until they had won the blue riband event of Gaelic football, the All-Ireland. However, this first victory did help to increase enthusiasm for the game in London, and a local London newspaper reported that 'football has become the craze here since the victory'.[19]

The History of the London GAA relates that Liam MacCarthy, a very successful businessman, 'lavishly entertained the football team later in London'.[20]

4

SAM MAGUIRE'S WORK FOR THE REPUBLICAN CAUSE IN LONDON

The IRB, the aim of which was to create a free and independent Ireland, was founded in Dublin on St Patrick's Day 1858. It was, in effect, an underground, revolutionary body. The renowned scholar John O'Mahony, who in 1858 helped found the Fenian Brotherhood, a fraternal republican organisation based in America with the same aims as the IRB, gave both organisations the umbrella name 'Fenians'. The name was derived from the legendary Irish band of warriors called the Fianna.

The IRB led an abortive rising in Ireland in 1867: nearly fifty years later the organisation was once again deeply involved in the planning of the Easter Rising. The Proclamation of 'The Provisional Government of the Irish Republic to the People of Ireland', issued during the Rising in Dublin, stated:

> Having organised and trained her manhood through her secret revolutionary organisation, the Irish Republican Brotherhood, and through her open military organisations, the Irish Volunteers and the Irish Citizen Army, having patiently perfected her discipline, having resolutely waited for the right moment to reveal itself, she now seizes that moment.[1]

The basic unit of the IRB was the circle, which was led by a centre. (In England, the circles were known as sections.) The ruling body was the Supreme Council, which claimed to be the government of the Republic (until it officially recognised Dáil Éireann in 1920). IRB members had been present at the founding meeting of the GAA in 1884 and continued to be a major, hidden influence on the organisation in the early years of its existence.

Brian Cusack, a member of the IRB, stated that in 1900 he had become 'a member of the Irish National Club which was really a cover for an I.R.B. Circle. This Circle held its meetings in a basement and as other social groups also held meetings there the I.R.B. organisation was not obvious.'[2] The Irish National Club's location – 55/56 Chancery Lane, London – was, as *The Irish in Britain 1815–1939* explains:

> ... the home of the Young Ireland Society (founded in 1882), Parnellite Leadership Committee (1891), Parnellite Irish National League of Great Britain (1891), Amnesty Association (1892), Gaelic League (1896), GAA (1895), ... Sinn Féin (1905).[3]

The success of Irish nationalist organisations in London was impressive. According to *The Irish in Britain*, 'By 1902 there were 1,500 members of the Gaelic League in London alone, with up to 50 Irish classes weekly in 14 schools.'[4] Many of the organisations had the same officers, who were all members of the IRB.[5] Dr Mark Ryan, president of the Irish National Club, was 'an old Fenian' and the leader (or head centre) of the IRB in London. The vice-president was Dr Anthony Mac-Bride, brother of Major John MacBride, who was executed for his role in the 1916 Rising. Indeed the Rising was largely planned by IRB members, who had successfully infiltrated the much larger body of Irish Volunteers (originally founded to fight for Home Rule rather than a republic) by recruiting many of its senior officers.

In 1902 Liam MacCarthy recruited Sam Maguire, who became a member of Cusack's branch of the IRB. Maguire, in turn, seems to have sworn in Michael Collins as a member of the organisation in 1909.[6] Collins later became the representative for the south of England on the IRB's Supreme

Council. Collins and Maguire would have known each other well during the former's time in London, as they had both worked in the post office when they first arrived from West Cork and both were members of the GAA.

Perhaps because of the constricted area in which they operated, there seems to have been a greater overlap between the Irish nationalist bodies in London than there was in Ireland. Peter Hart thought that:

> ... the [lack of] social distance between Maguire, a postal sorter, and Green [Alice Stopford Green], a literary salon-keeper and friend of cabinet ministers, illustrates the unusual egalitarianism of this world. A clear hierarchy remained however – this was Edwardian London after all. The overall tone was set by white and pink collar workers, junior civil servants in the main, with the post office to the fore.[7]

However, despite the greater integration, Hart quotes P. S. O'Hegarty to the effect that Irish labourers did not usually join the Gaelic League but would join the GAA. O'Hegarty later remembered of Maguire:

> Sam was a London Sorter. He and his two brothers, Dick and Jack – also Sorters – were amongst the foremost workers in London in the G.A.A. and in the I.R.B. They did not touch

the Gaelic League or Sinn Féin. Sam had been Secretary to the Divisional Executive of the I.R.B. from the time I joined it, and I felt fairly certain – though I had not seen him for years – that, after Dick Connolly's leaving London in 1918, Sam would have been the main force in the I.R.B.[8]

Membership in England of the IRB was estimated to be about 2,000 during the First World War.[9]

After the Easter Rising in 1916, when much of its leadership was executed, the IRB was reorganised under the leadership of Michael Collins, who was also a major player in the reorganisation of the Irish Volunteers. The Volunteers would become the IRA on the foundation of the first Dáil Éireann in 1919. Peter Hart described the relationship between the IRA and IRB in London:

The ever-growing demand for guns, ammunition and explosives [from Michael Collins in Ireland], and the infusion of young blood into the republican movement, led the I.R.B. to recruit new members from among the growing ranks of the Volunteers. The I.R.A in turn drew on recently formed Sinn Féin clubs and both recruited from the Irish Self-Determination League ... The Organisation [the I.R.B.] controlled them all from the start ... As many as half of the reliable Volunteers in London thereby became Organisation men.[10]

Indeed, Art O'Brien, the Dáil Representative in London, claimed that 'In so far as London was concerned, I.R.B. and I.R.A. were interchangeable terms.' According to Elizabeth McGinley, who was O'Brien's secretary:

> Sam Maguire, who was the key man in England for the purchase of arms for the Republican Army headquarters here, reported daily in person to the office. It was to him that the couriers from the various Republican government departments in Ireland reported ... He was a Post Office employee and knew Michael Collins very well. It was he who moulded him and initiated him into the whole idea of military republicanism. He was a wonderful man. I don't think he took five minutes of the twenty-four hours for himself. He spent it all working in some way for Ireland ... [And] he held all the reins of the whole movement in England in his hand.[11]

Peadar Kearney (writer of the Irish national anthem) recalled:

> It was evident that Sam Maguire was the ruling spirit [among London republicans]. Quiet to the verge of silence, he breathed earnestness and fixity of purpose. Far from being puritanical, he had a real sense of humour and could enter into a prank with the abandon of a schoolboy. If any of the boys had an inclination to cut loose, Sam's was the real steadying influence

that compelled the delinquent to think twice. All this was done firmly but quietly, with a smile that would 'coax birds off the bushes' ... those who did not know him personally must abide by the word of those who did. He was great in a generation that produced many such. Thank God.[12]

In 1918 Sam would have been the main point of contact and organiser for an audacious IRA operation. The UK government was contemplating the introduction of conscription of Irishmen into the British Army because of a shortage of men in the fight against Germany on the Western Front. A plan was put in place to assassinate members of the British government in the Houses of Parliament when, and if, it announced conscription in Ireland. The volunteers for these assassinations were told that it would be a 'suicide mission', but that their dependants and relatives would be provided for if they died.

Some time around April 1918 a group of fourteen volunteers travelled to London, where they met with Cathal Brugha (a prominent member of the Gaelic League, IRB and Irish Volunteers, who would later preside over the first meeting of the Dáil, on 21 January 1919, and be appointed Minister for Defence). They had to wait for the conscription act to be passed, and so spent many tense and tedious weeks in London. They met with Brugha on Hampstead Heath over the weeks and he would update them on what was happening. Then, one day, it seemed the time for the plan was near. Each man was required to draw a coloured bead from a hat – the chosen bead would indicate the target for that man. The volunteers were then given photographs of their intended victims. The plan was vague, but it seemed that the idea was to shoot their targets from the visitors' gallery in the House of Commons, although, as John Gaynor remarked, it was most unlikely that such a large number of men with Irish accents would gain access to the gallery. Brugha said it would not be possible to make a definite plan in advance. It was believed he had a source in Parliament who would let him know when David Lloyd George, the prime minister, would be making the announcement. When asked about an escape plan, Brugha said it was every man for himself. In mid-August the volunteers were issued with their weapons. However, the operation never took place, because although the UK government did pass the law that would allow conscription in Ireland, vociferous opposition from all sides of the political spectrum in Ireland, as well as prominent church members, meant that it was never introduced. The volunteers gave their guns back to Brugha and travelled individually back to Dublin.[13]

During the War of Independence, which broke out officially in January 1919, Sam's basic task in London for the

IRA was the interception of British government and military letters and telegrams. Piaras Béaslaí stated:

> Postal employees, as I have hinted, came to play a very big part in intelligence work. In London, the late Sam Maguire and his helpers organised an elaborate system of communication with the I.R.A., and of intercepting enemy communications. In Dublin – and even on mail boats – there was a body of workers operating in collaboration with the Intelligence Department. In various parts of the country, also, postal employees gave valuable assistance.[14]

Using sorters who worked on the mail train from Crewe (a major rail junction) to Dublin, Maguire set up a secure method of communication with Collins in Dublin. It was a very efficient system: a letter given to a sorter at Euston station in London at 6.30 p.m. would be delivered in Dublin at 7 a.m. the following day, and in many cases a reply would be received the following evening.

Elizabeth McGinley recalled that Sam 'reported daily in person to the [Sinn Féin] office [in London] ... He was at Euston station every morning to meet the couriers bringing letters from Ireland before he went to his own office.'[15] Richard Walsh, an IRA inspection officer, believed that 'Sam Maguire of London, who then held the rank of O/C [in the IRA] Britain ...[was] a sincere, energetic man.'[16] Joe Dolan (a member of Michael Collins' 'Squad'), in his witness statement, stated, 'Sam Maguire was the only one of the London crowd that I had much faith in that way [as a potential participant in IRA action in London]'.[17]

As well as intercepting important mails, Maguire ran an organisation for obtaining and smuggling arms, consisting of members of the IRA living in Britain. Michael Collins and Richard Mulcahy (the IRA's chief of staff) gave him this task at a meeting they had in London. The organisation had members in most of the big cities, and specifically in locations where there were military establishments – such as Aldershot, the headquarters of the British Army. The IRA also had members in the main ports, such as Liverpool and Bristol. On the Irish side of the channel, the main ports used were Dublin, Cork and Belfast.

It was made clear to all members, in addition to these specialist volunteers, that they should be on the lookout for opportunities to obtain weapons. The main sources of guns were arms dealers, pawnbrokers and gun clubs. But a special effort was made to get in touch with soldiers and sailors who might be willing to sell or steal weapons.

The Liverpool Battalion had a special section for handling this traffic. Richard Walsh described the method of smuggling weapons as follows: the IRA used a public house near the gates of Liverpool docks, which he described as being owned by a Jew 'married to an Irish Roman Catholic girl' who 'induced her husband' to allow the organisation to use it. The man bringing the weapons to be smuggled would go to the pub. Each weapon would be broken down into its component parts. Some of the parts were still quite bulky, but they could be hidden on a person of suitable proportions. The man would then pass through the gate to the docks to use the toilet and meet a man from the ship that was to carry the weapons. At the gate were several excise men and policemen, but for some odd reason they seem only to have been concerned with men coming from the docks and did not search those entering. The weapon components would be passed from the first to the second man. It was a very slow process, but it worked very well. On the ship, the person responsible for the weapons would have access to the ship's manifest, which described all the ship's cargo. A weapon would be placed in a suitable box or package – that is, one in which the extra weight would not be noticed. On arrival in an Irish port such as Dublin, the receiver would have a list of the boxes or packages that contained the weapons. These would be placed in a safe area where the IRA could access them and remove the weapons.[18]

The British were aware of this traffic and did their best to intercept the weapons. They searched passengers and every part of every ship that entered Irish ports, but, amazingly, they never searched the cargo. Richard Walsh suggested that this was because such a complex procedure would require a very large number of men, take a lot of time and thus interrupt commercial traffic. Further, if weapons were found the British could not bring charges against the firm or person to whom the goods were addressed. It was quite likely to be the case that such firms and people were pro-British.[19]

Another witness, James Delaney, gives a colourful description of his participation in arms smuggling:

> At the time I was familiar with two Irishmen named Lynch and Cooley. Both were ex-members of the London police, having been dismissed from the police force for going on strike. They put me in touch with a London Irishman, a bookmaker by the name of Conroy, as a man who might be able to procure arms for sale. Through Conroy I contacted a Jewman [*sic*] named Ginger Barnett in Petticoat Lane in the East End and a half-caste named Darby the Coon [*sic*]. The latter could best be described as a gang leader. Meanwhile, Tom Treacy had sent me £100 to start off with.
>
> With the assistance of Barnett and Darby the Coon, I would say that I managed to purchase two or three revolvers or automatics each week. Sometimes they sold them to me direct, but mostly, with one or the other, I visited sailors' lodging houses in Petticoat Lane, Limehouse Causeway, Pennyfields (Chinese quarter) and negro lodging houses in

Cable St. in the East End. Sailors whom I met in those places were the principal source of supply, and I paid anything from £2 to £4 for each revolver according to its size and condition.

I was staying at the time in a boarding house in Grosvenor Road near Victoria Station, but I never brought any of the revolvers there. As I got them I handed them over to a Kilkenny girl by the name of Annie O'Gorman who would be waiting to meet me at the Marble Arch. Later, in her residence, I would wrap the revolvers up in twelve yards of tailors' wadding and post the parcel to Kilkenny. I never sent more than one at a time. At first, in accordance with the arrangements I had made with Tom Treacy, I addressed the parcels to The Secretary, Electric Lighting Scheme, Town Hall, Kilkenny. This was, of course, a fictitious address, but the town clerk in Kilkenny, who knew nothing about the contents, had been advised by Tom Treacy or the late Leo Dardis to bring all parcels so addressed to the late Peter de Loughry in Parliament St. Later, on instructions from Treacy, I sent the parcels to other addresses in Kilkenny, including that of a cousin of my own.

This plan of purchasing the arms in London and getting them across worked well until November 1920. Then I was introduced by a most reliable Irish girl, who was a friend of Annie O'Gorman, to an Irishman whose name I cannot now recall. This man told me that there were a couple of hundred revolvers in a military store near Victoria Station. He said they were revolvers which had been handed in by Australian soldiers before their return to Australia; that he knew one of the storemen intimately and that the latter was prepared to bring out some of the revolvers and sell them. I told him that I would buy one after he said that he would act as the go-between between the storeman and myself. He got me one and after paying him for it, I had £50 on hands [*sic*], so I told him that I was prepared to take a further 25 at £2 each. He agreed and I made a further appointment to meet him again at 7 p.m. at Trafalgar Square. He was under the impression that I would bring the money and an empty suitcase for the guns to Trafalgar Square. He kept the appointment but I had neither the suitcase nor the money with me. After greeting me, he excused himself for a moment and crossed the road. I was immediately apprehended by two detectives who came from behind me. They searched me and then took me to Scotland Yard. One of the detectives was Chief Inspector McGrath of the C.I.D. [Criminal Investigation Department]. He questioned me for four hours and took a statement from me, in which I denied point blank that I had any interest in purchasing arms except that I was going to Belfast and that, if I could get it, I was prepared to buy one revolver to protect myself from both sides while in Belfast. He took my keys and my address and I was then put in a cell in Canning St. police station.

The next morning I was taken again to McGrath's office. He handed me back my keys and £50 which I had locked up in my suitcase in my room of the boarding house in Grosvenor

Road and told me I was free to go. They (the C.I.D.) had searched my room during the night but had found nothing which would in any way incriminate me. At the time I had seven revolvers with Annie O'Gorman.

The first thing I did after leaving Scotland Yard was to change my digs from Grosvenor Road to ones in Edgeware Road. I also decided to leave London and to go home to Kilkenny. I got in touch with Miss O'Gorman and met her at the Marble Arch, when I explained the position to her. I told her I would take three of the revolvers with me, and I asked her to wrap up the other four exactly as she had seen me do it and to post them singly to addresses in Kilkenny which I gave her.

One of the revolvers which I took with me was a Webley Service revolver and I fasted [*sic*] it between the back buttons of my trousers with the barrel pointing up my back. Another was a short Parabellum, which I broke down into its component parts and sewed them into the hem at the bottom of my overcoat. The third was a small 32 automatic, and this I sewed into a shoulder pad of my overcoat. I travelled via Holyhead and Dún Laoghaire, and except that my luggage was searched at Holyhead I reached Kilkenny without incident, where I handed over the three revolvers to Tom Treacy and gave him an account of what had happened to me in London. As regards the four revolvers which I had left behind with Miss O'Gorman, one reached its destination safely. The second one she sent reached the sorting office in the post office, Kilkenny. Here a post office assistant named O'Driscoll saw the butt of it protruding from the wadding and wrapping. He handed the parcel over to the Postmaster, who reported it to the R.I.C. [Royal Irish Constabulary]. It was addressed to a girl in the Cloth Hall, Kilkenny, who knew nothing about it beyond the fact that when the parcel arrived she was to hand it over to Kieran Tobin, who was then a Volunteer officer in Kilkenny. This discovery led to the girl's arrest, and it must also have led to the discovery in the post of the other two, for although both were posted in London by Miss O'Gorman they were never delivered in Kilkenny. Thus finished until after the Truce the purchasing of arms by me for the I.R.A.[20]

Many witnesses report that this central organisation for procuring weapons, despite being well funded, was not very effective. This led to many IRA brigades sending their own agents to England to get weapons, which caused tension between the IRA headquarters and these brigades. One Mayo quartermaster had his consignment confiscated by the headquarters even though he had Michael Collins' permission to obtain them and the weapons ended up being sent to a brigade in Cork.[21]

On 12 August 1920 Terence MacSwiney – lord mayor of Cork and officer commanding (O/C) 1st Battalion, Cork IRA – was arrested for having seditious documents and an RIC key for deciphering coded messages. He was sentenced to two years' imprisonment and became a prisoner in Brixton Prison, where he began a hunger strike to obtain prisoner-of-war rather than criminal status. Michael Collins decided to launch a rescue attempt; four volunteers were sent to London and made contact with Sam Maguire. However, the attempt was aborted because it was deemed to be impossible.

Collins then asked Pa Murray to carry out a mission to kill some members of the British Cabinet as an act of revenge in the event of MacSwiney's death. Collins told him to go to London and there make contact with Maguire, 'who would have more detailed instructions'. He travelled to London with two other volunteers, Jack Cody and Con Sullivan. They met with Maguire, who arranged accommodation for them and money to pay their expenses. Maguire also introduced Murray to Reginald (Reggie) Dunne (O/C London IRA), who arranged for Murray to inspect the London IRA companies, under the guise of a representative from headquarters, to select men who would be suitable for the task.[22]

Collins instructed him to let Maguire know in advance about any plan for action that he might develop, but nothing was to be attempted before MacSwiney died. And, Murray explains in his witness statement, 'If I did succeed in doing anything, Collins could hold out no hope that myself or any man taking part in the action would be rescued [survive it].'[23]

Murray and Dunne arranged for intelligence to be gathered about the movements of the chosen ministers. In particular, they were interested in discovering whether or not there was a regular pattern in their movements. Cody, who was to be the driver, familiarised himself with driving conditions in London. Having studied the ministers' movements for a few weeks, they found they were irregular and unpredictable, so it would not be possible to put the plan into action. Michael Collins, when informed of the lack of viability of the plan, said that something should be done.

Murray decided to attempt to assassinate Arthur Balfour, a leading conservative politician who had earned the nickname 'Bloody Balfour' during his time as Irish secretary because of his strict enforcement of coercive legislation.[24] It was discovered that Balfour would be going to Oxford on a Tuesday in mid-October. Murray sent his proposal to Collins, who did not give permission and recalled the volunteers to Dublin. Despite this command, Murray went to Oxford, where he met Balfour in the street and approached him to ask him for directions to one of the Oxford colleges. Balfour provided him with the directions and said, 'You are an Irish man?' to which Murray replied, 'Yes', and continued on his way. Murray points out that Balfour did not have an armed guard.[25]

On his return to Dublin the following Thursday, Murray says, Collins told him he was sorry, but that he could not risk having anything happen until MacSwiney died. At the end of the story, Murray pays tribute to the London Volunteers, of whom he says the majority appeared to be civil servants.[26] Terence MacSwiney died on 25 October 1920.

Despite the fact that none of these proposed assassinations were carried out in England during the War of Independence, alternative action was taken. Throughout the conflict British forces in Ireland burned houses, creameries and other forms of property as reprisals, and Michael Collins decided that the IRA should conduct a similar campaign in England. He sent a volunteer named George Fitzgerald, who described the events in November 1920.[27] Fitzgerald reported that he contacted Sam Maguire and Reggie Dunne when he arrived in London. Fitzgerald's role was to plan the campaign by selecting suitable targets, typically warehouses, which had viable escape routes. The attacks were to take place on Saturday night, around midnight, because the streets would be very crowded and it would be possible for the volunteers to mingle with the crowds to avoid capture.

The proposed method was that the volunteers would enter the basements of the targeted warehouses to be burned by cutting a window with a diamond cutter after putty attached to paper had been attached to the window. This technique was used to prevent the glass falling on the ground, shattering and making a noise that might attract attention.

On the night, Fitzgerald and Maguire walked to the district where the buildings were located. They expected several buildings to be on fire following a successful operation, but they did not see any fires. Fitzgerald concluded that the 'London Volunteers hadn't been used to this kind of work [and] they cried off at the last minute.' Quite sensibly, Fitzgerald decided to give them practice at this 'kind of work'. He took them into the country outside London, and they burned several large haystacks on farms in different areas. Fitzgerald states, 'This plan was successful as quite a large quantity of hay was destroyed in several farms.' The result was what he calls 'a number of minor burning activities on the outskirts of London, particularly Railway Signal Boxes'. Despite Fitzgerald's use of the word 'minor', the British authorities were concerned enough about these burnings to erect 'several barricades in Whitehall and Downing Street'.[28]

In Liverpool and Manchester similar campaigns were carried out. The initial plan of the Liverpool volunteers was to blow up the dock gates in Liverpool harbour – gates necessary because at low water there could be a difference of twenty-five feet between the water level in the river and that in the docks. The details of this plan were discovered in a raid in Dublin, so the operation was cancelled.

On Saturday 27 November 1920 fourteen cotton warehouses and four large timber yards were burned in Liverpool and Manchester. The local newspapers reported that the damage amounted to hundreds of thousands of pounds sterling, and the police were overwhelmed by requests for protection of offices and warehouses.[29]

These volunteers also burned hay on farms in the Liverpool area and attacked the homes of men serving in Ireland as Black and Tans (made up largely of ex-army men who had fought in the First World War recruited by the British government in an attempt to combat the IRA) or Auxiliaries (a special force of ex-British Army officers, categorised as 'auxiliary' police officers). Hugh Early, commandant of the Liverpool Volunteers, says in his BMH statement that nine houses were raided and two were burned.[30]

At the end of 1920 the IRA in Dublin was attacking the British forces by throwing grenades into the vehicles transporting British soldiers. To prevent this practice, the military decided to carry captured TDs in the vehicles. The TD would be handcuffed when he was in the lorry. In retaliation, the IRA decided to arrest twelve members of the British government, including ministers if possible. Once again, headquarters sent volunteers to England to carry out the operation: Frank Thornton, Seán Flood and George Fitzgerald.[31]

On arrival the men made contact with Sam Maguire and Reggie Dunne. As with the operation to avenge the death of Terence MacSwiney, the IRA studied the habits of MPs who supported the Conservative–Liberal government led by David Lloyd George. In contrast to what had happened during the other operation, this time the unit was able to identify twenty-five members who had predictable habits and was also able to discover 'some very interesting side-lights ... on the private lives of members of the British Government'.[32]

The IRA unit drew up a detailed plan that included houses where the hostages were to be kept; transport was ready and all the necessary information was available. They reported this to headquarters in Dublin. However, in the meantime, the British Army had stopped the practice of carrying hostages in their trucks, so headquarters called off the operation. Thornton was relieved, but he said he was confident that the unit could have successfully implemented the plan.

One day when Thornton and Flood were entering Westminster station to take a train to Acton, they saw that the gates were just closing. Flood offered to race Thornton. The route contained three bends; Flood ran ahead, and when Thornton came around the second-last bend he found that Flood had run into a man and both of them had fallen to the ground. Flood and Thornton helped to get the man on his feet. To their surprise, two men who were with him produced revolvers and ordered them to put their hands up; however, they ignored this command and continued to 'brush down the man' who had been knocked over. Then they discovered the man was Lloyd George, the British prime minister. The first thing he did was to tell his guards to put away their guns, but they were slow to do that, because they recognised the Irish accents and thought Lloyd George might be in danger.

He then said, 'Well, Irishmen or no Irishmen, if they were out to shoot me I was shot long ago.' Having apologised to Lloyd George, Flood and Thornton continued their journey. However, they did not go to Acton, but instead took a train going in the opposite direction and got off at the next station to check that they were not being followed.[33]

During the War of Independence (1919–1921) most units of the British Army behaved reasonably well, certainly by contrast with the actions of the Black and Tans and the Auxiliaries. One exception was the Essex Regiment stationed in West Cork. A prominent officer in this regiment was Major Percival. Tom Barry describes him as 'easily the most viciously anti-Irish of all serving British officers … Day and night he raided homes and arrested numbers, including some who had no connection with the IRA.'[34] His men captured and tortured two IRA men, Tom Hales and Pat Harte, in July 1920. The officers who interrogated and tortured Hales beat him and crushed most of his teeth with pliers, but Hales refused to give any information. Both prisoners had their fingernails pulled out and were subjected to a mock execution by a firing squad. The torture was so severe that Pat Harte suffered a mental breakdown.[35] He did not recover and died in the mental hospital in Cork in February 1924.

In October 1920 Barry discovered that on three consecutive nights Percival had walked a short distance from the barracks in Bandon, County Cork, to a house for dinner at 7.45 p.m. On the fourth night, Barry and members of his unit waited to assassinate Percival, but he did not appear. It later turned out he was away from Bandon, raiding houses.

The West Cork Brigade then discovered that Percival would be taking a holiday to Dovercourt, a small seaside resort on the coast of Essex. Michael Collins sent Frank Thornton, Bill Ahearne, Pa Murray and Tadhg O'Sullivan to England to shoot Percival. When they arrived in London, they met Maguire and Reggie Dunne. Frank Thornton describes the situation as 'unhealthy', because of the campaign of reprisals being undertaken by the IRA in England. They discovered that Percival was staying in the military barracks in Dovercourt and it was not possible to shoot him. However, they learned that he would be returning to Ireland on 16 March via Liverpool Street Station. Thornton's group, together with additional men from the London IRA, were waiting for Percival.[36]

Thornton recalled:

At a quarter to three we were amazed to see Sam Maguire standing by the side of the News Kiosk beckoning one of us to come over to him. Now Sam had never shown his hand in London before for very good reasons as he was our principal Intelligence Officer there, but on this occasion his hand was forced because one of his contacts in Scotland Yard had given him the tip that the C.I.D. had spotted some of our party and that all preparations were made to surround the Station ... Needless to remark, we got out as quickly as possible ... We learned afterwards that at about five minutes to three a cordon of military and police was thrown around the station and every passenger had to pass through the cordon ... The unfortunate part about it was that Percival was able to get back to Cork safely.[37]

Thornton accompanied Tadhg O'Sullivan to Liverpool and put him on a coal boat going to Cork. Then, he says, when he returned to Dublin the following night:

I bought the 'Herald' on my way up to O'Connell Bridge, and to my amazement saw right across the top of the paper 'Tadhg Sullivan [sic] shot dead in Cork', and the irony of it is that he was shot dead in a raid carried out by Percival on a house in Cork. This was on 19th April, 1921. It appears from what I found out afterwards that a meeting of one of the City Battalion Councils was being held and Tadhg on arrival at the house, spotted the raiding party before he went in, and so as to draw them away from the meeting made a dash across the road into another building and was shot dead in attempting to escape through the back window of a house.[38]

Although Percival escaped his fate on this occasion, Sam Maguire was apparently involved in another assassination in England, this one successful. One of the greatest challenges for any Irish revolutionary movement was British spies, and it was one of these who met their fate in London. According to Joseph Kinsella:

> When I left the Battalion, Dublin IRA, temporarily to deal with munitions under Seán Russell, Vincent Fouvargue was appointed Intelligence Officer of the 4th Battalion, which appointment he held for about three or four weeks. On handing over I gave him very little information about his duties, or about who he was to contact. From the outset I personally did not place a lot of trust in him, because on the morning that he took over from me he appeared to me to be too inquisitive about the movements of Michael Collins and the G.H.Q. [General Headquarters] staff generally. He wanted to know where they could be located at any time. He said that he had big things in view, and that it would be to the advantage of the movement generally if he was in a position to get in touch with the principal men with the least possible

delay. From his attitude I there and then formed the opinion, rightly or wrongly, that he was inclined to overstep his position. I did not feel too happy about him and I discussed him with Seán Dowling.

It transpired that my impressions of this man were correct. I told him of two meeting places of the Intelligence staff, one of Company Intelligence held at Rathmines Road and one of Brigade Intelligence held at Seville Place. A short time after giving him this information, both these places were raided. I suspected him then and sent my suspicions to Intelligence. Whatever action was taken then was taken by them. The Black and Tans raided the Company Intelligence meeting and the whole staff, I think there were eight or nine of them, were arrested.

I was on my way to Seville Place to warn the Brigade Intelligence Officer that the place might be raided, but I was met and turned back by the 3rd Battalion Intelligence Officer, Geoff Keating. The hall in Seville Place was raided, but there was nobody in it. Some papers were got in the raid, and as a result the Brigade Intelligence Officer, Peter Ennis, was arrested a few days afterwards. I think he got two years' imprisonment. He was badly beaten up, and all his teeth were knocked down his throat. He was Tom Ennis's brother.

I was now confirmed in my suspicions that Fouvargue was giving away information and that he was responsible for the raids and for the arrests. Fouvargue knew that the British had acted directly on his orders and he also knew that suspicion would fall on him immediately. I do not know what transpired later but apparently he was arrested for his own protection. Some time following his arrest, he was taken out with some other prisoners one night in a lorry. When the lorry stopped on the South Circular Road, Dolphins Barn, to question somebody passing by, Fouvargue jumped from it and escaped.[39]

Fouvargue left Dublin for London, where he was shot on a golf course by Joe Shanahan and Reggie Dunne.[40]

Fouvargue was not the only spy to be exposed and dealt with during the War of Independence. In the early morning of 23 March 1921, six members of 'C' Company, 1st Battalion, Cork No. 1 Brigade were shot by a party of Black and Tans and RIC at a farm at Ballycannon, Clogheen, just outside Cork city. The IRA believed that Patrick Connors had betrayed them. Connors was part of the Ballingeary flying column under the command of Seán O'Hegarty that carried out the Coolavokig Ambush on British forces on 25 February. After the ambush Connors had returned to Cork and was later arrested by the RIC for the possession of a revolver. The IRA believed that Connors broke down under interrogation and betrayed the men who were shot.[41]

Daniel Healy states that just before the truce of July 1921 he was in Cork and was informed by a battalion officer that Connors would be collecting a letter at Hammersmith post office. Healy and Liam O'Callaghan went to London to shoot him when he arrived at the post office. En route through Dublin they met Michael Collins, who gave them a note for Sam Maguire. They arrived in London on 10 July 1921 and met Maguire, who passed them on to Seán Flood. Over a period of ten days, they waited near Hammersmith post office, but they did not see Connors. Concluding that the attempt was a failure, they returned to Cork.[42] In 1922 the IRA succeeded in assassinating Connors in New York city, where he had moved in an attempt to escape retribution.

The Aftermath of the War of Independence

In *The IRA in Britain, 1919–1923* Gerard Noonan summarises the campaign the IRA began in late 1920:

> In November 1920, with the burning of warehouses and timber yards on Merseyside, the IRA began a campaign of violence in Britain ... Over the course of the subsequent seven and a half months, Volunteers mounted at least 239 operations, mainly taking the form of burning property. Targets included farms, factories, warehouses, communications and railway infrastructure situated in and around the cities of Liverpool, Manchester, Newcastle-upon-Tyne and Glasgow. RIC men and their relatives were also attacked and a number

of attempts were made to assassinate and kidnap politicians, soldiers and policemen.[43]

The campaign finished when the Truce came into force on 11 July 1921. Rory O'Connor, director of operations for the IRA in England, thought it was quite successful. Michael Collins obviously concurred in this assessment, as he later told Sam Maguire and others that in October 1921, at the start of negotiations for the Treaty, Lloyd George said the British government was more afraid of the London unit than all the IRA units active in Ireland combined.

Charles Townshend, author of several books on the period, has written that 'some form of military struggle was inevitable before Irish demands would be taken seriously'.[44] Taking the war to Britain acted as a support for the struggle in Ireland. Sam Maguire, leader of the IRB in London, supported Michael Collins; during the negotiations for the Anglo-Irish Treaty late in 1921 Maguire made sure that he was in constant contact with the IRB Supreme Council by travelling home every weekend to Dublin.

On 3 December 1921 Collins was met by the IRB secretary Seán Ó Muirthile at Dún Laoghaire for a very brief meeting. Collins then went to a Dáil Cabinet meeting to discuss the Treaty. While the Cabinet was meeting, the IRB council was also in session. At a lunch break, Collins met the IRB secretary again. The IRB had three areas of concern about the proposed Treaty with Britain:

1   The oath of allegiance to the crown.

2   Britain remaining in several ports around Ireland, that is, the British navy would retain the right to use the ports such as Castletownbere and Cobh (Queenstown) in Cork and Lough Swilly. These were known as the 'Treaty ports'.

3   The proposal for the partition of Ulster with a separate government for six counties.

However, the council agreed to accept the latest version of the oath of allegiance:

I ……. do solemnly swear true faith and allegiance to the Constitution of the Irish Free State as by law established and that I will be faithful to H.M. King George V., his heirs and successors by law, in virtue of the common citizenship of Ireland with Great Britain and her adherence to and membership of the group of nations forming the British Commonwealth of Nations.[45]

It also left the question of the Treaty ports to the discretion of the delegation conducting the negotiations. On the question of the partition of Ulster, Collins agreed that he would refuse to accept it and would attempt to ensure that if a breakdown occurred in the negotiations it would be over the issue of Ulster.

Shortly after the Treaty was signed on 6 December 1921, the IRB council met to decide on the organisation's attitude to the document. Opinion was divided. Most members were pleased that the organisation's version of the oath had been accepted but were not happy about the Treaty ports. The crux of the issue was still the situation in Ulster, where pogroms against nationalists were taking place. Collins said that in his opinion the Northern Ireland government would collapse in two or three years (it was assumed at that point that it would not be economically viable because the nationalist areas/counties would be excluded and the remaining state would be very small). During that time, he suggested that the new National Army be based primarily on the flying columns to a total of 20,000 men. Presumably, the implication was that military action could be taken to unify the country.

Although the proposal to accept the Treaty was opposed by Liam Lynch, a member of the council, commander of the Cork No. 2 Brigade of the IRA during the War of Independence and, later, commander of the IRA's 1st Southern Division, at the end of the discussion the council decided that the IRB would endorse the Treaty. But rather than force anyone into a decision, a short time later the secretary wrote to members who were also TDs to tell them they were free to make the choice to vote for or against the Treaty when the question came before the Dáil.[46]

On 12 December 1921 the council sent a letter to all the centres of the IRB, which said that the organisation was adopting a neutral position with regards to the Treaty. It also referred to the organisation's traditional perspective, which 'was to make use of all instruments, political or military, which related to attaining freedom and an independent Ireland'.[47] However, the IRB ultimately split over the Treaty. The strongest opposition came from Munster and Connacht. It was alleged that some IRB centres who were opposed to the Treaty did not circulate the statement of neutrality by the ruling body to its members.

Like the IRB, the IRA also split over the Treaty, and by early 1922 the two sides were on a collision course that would quickly lead to Civil War. Sam Maguire chose to remain loyal to Michael Collins and support the Treaty, so various men who were sent to London by the anti-Treaty IRA at this time to obtain weapons stated that they deliberately avoided making contact with him.

The catalyst for the Civil War came in June 1922. Sir Henry Wilson had ended the First World War as the most senior British soldier, chief of the Imperial General Staff.

During the War of Independence, he advocated a very strong military response against the Irish. When Lloyd George began negotiations with the Irish, Wilson accused him of betrayal, resigned from the army and was elected as a Unionist MP for a Northern Ireland constituency in North Down. He also acted as the security adviser to the new Northern Ireland government, formed under the Government of Ireland Act in 1920 which split the country in two. It was because of this role that he was blamed by many people in the newly created Free State for pogroms against nationalists, particularly with the creation of the B Specials – a part-time group of 20,000 men within a new police force created in Northern Ireland in October 1921 because the Ulster Unionist leaders did not think that the RIC could be relied on to be loyal to the new Unionist government there.

On 22 June 1922 Sir Henry went to Liverpool Street Station in London to unveil a war memorial. Two IRA men, London O/C Reggie Dunne and volunteer Joseph O'Sullivan, were present; they intended to assassinate Wilson. However, they thought there were too many people present, so decided to wait for another opportunity. When Wilson returned to his home, Eaton Place, later in the afternoon, they were waiting for him. He paid for his taxi and began to walk to the door of his house. As he climbed his steps, they shot him dead.

Both Dunne and O'Sullivan had served in the British

Army during the First World War. O'Sullivan had lost a leg at the battle of Ypres; his wooden leg slowed down their escape on the day of the assassination. Despite the fact that they wounded a policeman and two civilians, they were captured by a large, angry crowd, who wanted immediate revenge for the killing, and had to be rescued by the police. Both men were convicted and sentenced to hang.

There is a continuing controversy about whether this action was authorised by Dublin, and in particular, by Michael Collins. There is no direct evidence that Maguire was involved in this affair, but there is a suggestion that his departure from London in 1923 may have been due to a Scotland Yard investigation to find out if he was involved.

Joe Dolan, a member of Michael Collins' 'Squad', reports in his witness statement that Collins instructed him to travel to London to examine the feasibility of a rescue of Dunne and O'Sullivan. He was told to report to Maguire in London, and the two met at Peele's public house in Fetter Lane, off Fleet Street, 'the usual place where Maguire could be contacted'.[48]

Maguire was aware of Dolan's mission and got a London IRA intelligence man named Seán Golden to show him around and assist him as necessary. Dolan determined that the best prospect for a rescue would be when the men were being transported from Wandsworth jail to the courthouse. He returned to Dublin to report to Collins; he told him that he did not think the London volunteers, with the sole exception of Sam Maguire ('the only one of the London crowd that I had much faith in that way'), were capable of carrying out the operation. He said it would be possible if members of the 'Squad' or the Dublin active service unit were used for the operation.[49]

Later in his statement Dolan says:

> But some time afterwards I met Sam Maguire – that was long after the execution of Dunne and O'Sullivan – and we discussed my last visit to him in London and my mission there. He told me that, subsequent to my visit, Tom Cullen had come over to London with apparently the mission from Collins of checking on my report. Whether Tom Cullen reported adversely on the possibility of carrying out the rescue or not, I do not know, but Sam Maguire remarked to me that the job could easily have been done if it had been left to me but that when Cullen came over, he could not see it the way I did and the attempt was consequently abandoned.[50]

5

RETURN TO DUBLIN AND DISMISSAL

The initiative for the return of Sam Maguire to work in the post office in Ireland came from P. S. O'Hegarty, who was secretary of the Department of Posts and Telegraphs:

> Some time later in 1922 it was conveyed to me that it would be a good thing to transfer Sam to Dublin. There were then a number of vacancies in the Dublin Sorting Office, due to men who preferred to go to England, and there were, of course, large numbers of applicants from the other side. The general arrangements had not been settled, but I arranged for Sam's transfer specially ...[1]

According to the *History of the London GAA*:

> Earlier in the year [1923] Sam Maguire had slipped quietly

out of London. There was no big announcement; the only record is a pocket watch now in the Croke Park museum which was presented to him by the London County Board in February.[2]

Various sources claimed that Maguire left London with a substantial pension of between £3,000–£4,000.[3] However, there is no record of such a pension, as this report by an archives assistant indicates:

The British Postal Museum & Archive

Report on the post office employment of Samuel Maguire:

Thank you for your order for research into the post office career of Samuel Maguire.

Using the information you provided, I began by searching the Appointment indexes. I located a record of an appointment (Copy A) of a Samuel Maguire as a Sorter in 1897 at 'London CO', or London Central Office. Appointment records sometimes show when individuals received promotions, pay rises or moved regions, but not consistently, so we cannot infer anything about Mr Maguire's subsequent service from the fact that he only appears once in these.

Next I searched the Pension & Gratuity Indexes for the year 1923, the year you stated that he retired, but I was unable to find a mention of Mr Maguire in these. In case he was listed mistakenly as 'McGuire' I checked for this name too, but I could find no mention of a 'Samuel McGuire' either. I then expanded my search to the years 1924 to 1927, but unfortunately I could still not find a record of a pension award to him.

I searched through the staff magazine, St Martin's Le Grand, for the years 1922–1927 but I could not locate a mention of Mr Maguire's retirement or death. Likewise, I sadly could not find a mention of him in the staff Establishment books, which list the more senior grades.

Ashley March
Archives Assistant
06/07/2015

Further, Barry Attoe of the UK post office archive stated:

I have done a quick search and there is an entry for a Samuel Maguire appointed as a sorter in the Controllers Office in London, November 1898. Unusually, there is a note in the margin next to his name: 'cancelled for Dublin 8/3/23'.

And:

Once again, I must advise you that Samuel Maguire does not appear in the pension and gratuity records we have here ...

However, from the information you have given it sounds as though he left the post office of his own accord, before retirement.[4]

There is also a significant problem with the figure of £3,000–£4,000. The value of this sum would be approximately £150,000–£200,000 in 2017. It is not credible that a postal sorter would be paid such a large sum of money in 1923 or any year. Maguire had approximately twenty-five years of service in 1923, and it is reasonably safe to assume that full service to retire with a pension would require at least forty years, or an even longer period. This would seem to suggest that he did not receive a pension when he left the UK post office.

When Maguire returned to Ireland he went to work as a clerical officer in the office of Minister for Posts and Telegraphs J. J. Walsh, from Bandon, another West Cork man, who would have known him from their IRB days in London.

An important event that occurred in 1924 was the mutiny in the National Army. When the force was created in 1922 to be the army of the new Irish Free State, it was quickly faced with the Civil War and the fight against the anti-Treaty forces – sometimes known as the 'irregulars'. Due to the overriding need to win this war, the army recruited many men and officers who had served in the British Army. Michael Collins placed a high value on their training and experience. When he appointed the top commanders of the National Army, he chose men who were members of the IRB, including Richard Mulcahy, Gearóid O'Sullivan and Seán MacMahon. Perhaps surprisingly, he did not choose the men who had served in his 'Squad' during the War of Independence, such as Liam Tobin and Charles Dalton.

By the end of the Civil War, the army had more than 50,000 soldiers and 3,000 officers. To put this into perspective, in 2017 the army had about 9,000 officers and men. The country did not need and could not afford the cost of such a large army once the conflict had ended, so a process of demobilisation began, with the aim of reducing the army by two-thirds. It was also decided to make the army more professional.

The situation in the lead-up to the mutiny is best described by J. Bowyer Bell:

Many of those who had taken the Treaty side had done so in loyalty to Collins or in hopes that the Free State would be a stepping-stone to a Republic. Collins was dead [killed in an ambush on 22 August 1922 at Béal na Bláth, Co. Cork] and the Cabinet seemed to be wedded to a narrow interpretation of the Treaty. More irritating, the army had kept former British professional soldiers and demobilised the Old IRA men … The glory days had gone to be replaced by ministers in three-piece suits quibbling over pension plans and licensing laws.[5]

These 'Old IRA men' objected to the revival of the IRB – described by Bell as 'a new IRB' – by senior members of the Free State Army Council, including Minister of Defence Richard Mulcahy. They felt they were being excluded from the revived IRB and thus were at a disadvantage when it came to demobilisation, as they believed that officers who were members of this revived IRB would be allowed to remain in the army, while they would not.

On 29 January 1923 they formed the Irish Republican Army Organisation (IRAO), also known as the Old IRA. On 6 March 1924 two members of the organisation, Liam Tobin and Charles Dalton, issued an ultimatum to the government. They demanded that the government dismiss the members of the army council – the leadership of the army – and stop the process of demobilisation, as due to the poor state of the economy there were few jobs available for those who had to leave the army.

The government responded by temporarily placing Eoin O'Duffy (the garda commissioner) in charge of the army and dismissing Richard Mulcahy because he had allowed the IRB to be revived and given that organisation a significant role in the army. The government regarded the mutineers as having rejected the lawful authority of the army and the government. As in many western democratic states, the government believed that the army was the servant of the government and should not involve itself in politics. (This is in contrast to the situation pertaining in other countries, where the army views intervention in national politics as a right and is willing to stage a coup if it considers the government is not good for the country. A classic example is that of the Turkish army, which regards itself as the guardian of the secular Turkish republic and has overthrown governments that it has perceived to be deviating towards a religious republic.)

It seems that, although he was not a member of the army, Maguire was a member of the IRAO. Several historians state that he advocated violence when the other members of the IRAO were actually willing to compromise with the government. For example, John M. Regan says:

> Soldiers obeyed politicians, even politicians arguably in the wrong, and so Mulcahy and the other generals deserve the plaudits which have been given to them as essentially good democrats. The IRAO also conformed with remarkable speed to the wishes of the civil government they had repudiated. There was so much potential for violence, all sides sought to avoid it … The only real incitement to violence from within the IRAO came not from the soldiers but from a civilian member, Sam Maguire … Maguire in the period immediately after the mutiny advocated that the IRAO should assassinate members of the Executive Council and senior army officers.[6]

The suggestion of Maguire's participation is supported by the BMH witness statement of Elizabeth McGinley, who had worked for Sinn Féin in London and knew Maguire:

> I think it was on the 11th November 1923 [Armistice Day on which the dead of the First World War are commemorated], I met him coming out from his job in the Castle and the whole city was decorated with Union Jacks. He said, 'Isn't this a dreadful sight. This is the result of all our hard work and sacrifices. This is the last time this will happen, I guarantee. This is not what the people who signed the Treaty intended. [This was a reference to Michael Collins.] The Treaty is not being worked the way they expected. When I have a talk with the boys we'll see that the Treaty is properly enforced.' He evidently got in touch with the group in the Army who were dissatisfied with the way things were going and who afterwards mutinied.[7]

Despite this allegation, Maguire was not immediately dismissed from his post in the civil service. But on 29 December 1924 the secretary of the Department of Posts and Telegraphs received a letter that stated 'the Executive Council [the official title of the Free State government] has ordered the dismissal from the Public Service of Mr Samuel Maguire, a clerical officer in the Department of Posts and Telegraphs'. By way of explanation, the letter stated that:

... the Executive Council has reason to believe the person concerned has been in close and active association with a conspiracy. The object of which to suborn from their allegiance members of the army and other State Services with a view to renewing the attempt to subject the Government to pressure of an unconstitutional nature.

I am to request that you will take steps immediately on receipt of this letter to notify Mr Maguire of his dismissal. No payment of salary should be made to him for any period subsequent to this date.[8]

On 30 December 1924 Maguire received the following letter:

A Chara

I am directed by the Minister for Finance [Ernest Blythe] to inform you that the Executive Council have ordered your immediate dismissal from the Public Service.

You are therefore now relieved from duty.

J. B.

[James Banam, secretary to the president of the Executive Council][9]

On 9 March 1925 Maguire wrote to his friend J. J. Walsh, the Minister of Posts and Telegraphs:

On 30 December 1924 I was dismissed from the Public Service of the Irish Free State by order of the Executive Council without any definite charge brought against me. I have already written two letters to the secretary of the Executive Council requesting that the reason for my dismissal be definitely stated and that I be given a chance of answering the same. Up to the present I have received no reply and in consequence I am writing to you as the Official Head of my Department if you could supply the reason for my dismissal.

(Signed) S. Maguire. Late C.O. [clerical officer][10]

On 11 March J. J. Walsh sent a letter to the president, W. T. Cosgrave. Walsh said that while the government had the right to dismiss a civil servant without giving a reason, it was not normal practice and that dismissal without an opportunity to answer the charges occurred only when 'the officer concerned has been guilty of an illegality'. He argued that the case should be reconsidered because of Maguire's excellent work for Michael Collins and on compassionate grounds. He stated that Maguire had at an earlier point in his life suffered from tuberculosis and was not in a fit condition to cope with 'the rough and tumble of a fresh start in life at the age of 48'. Finally he said Maguire had assured him that he was not involved in any illegality and Walsh was willing to accept that assurance. He promised that 'if he is reinstated he will serve the Government loyally in all respects'.[11]

Mr Banam requested the views of Diarmuid O'Hegarty, secretary to the Executive Council. O'Hegarty replied on 19 May 1925:

> The action was taken as a result of reports submitted by Army Intelligence – copies of these were not circulated.
>
> There can be no doubt of the very great services rendered by Mr Maguire during the period before the Treaty. My memory does not go back as far as 1902, but certainly since 1916 Maguire was one of the leading workers in London.
>
> At the time of the Army Split Maguire made himself prominent with the Tobin–Dalton group and as far as I can recollect his name appears as one of the signatories to a letter by them regarding the return of stolen arms which was published in their pamphlet THE TRUTH ABOUT THE ARMY CRISIS.
>
> I have not any knowledge of Maguire's connections with that organisation since that date. He was naturally on terms of very close personal friendship with a number of the mutineers and doubtless continued to associate with them in public. Maguire is an able man and so far as I know could be relied upon if he gave his word to keep it.
>
> Contrary to the statement made in his letter to the Secretary of the post office, no letters were received in this office from him asking the reason for his dismissal.[12]

On 30 April J. J. Walsh wrote again, appealing for generosity to Sam Maguire because of his very poor circumstances, as he did not have a job and therefore no income. The letter also appealed on behalf of another dismissed employee, Seán Milroy:

> I understand that there is a fund at your disposal which may be called upon in extreme cases of this kind, that you may be so kind as to advance a small sum, say one hundred pounds each. I believe this would be merely an act of charity.
> J. J. Walsh[13]

The request was granted, and a cheque for £100 was sent to Sam Maguire on 2 May 1925. Another payment of £100 was made on 23 April 1926. (The amount of £100 in that period would be equivalent to €5,482 in 2016.)

Elizabeth McGinley recalled:

> Sam told me that Kevin O'Higgins was informed of all this sort of work that was going on by a member of the Department of Defence who was placed there for the purpose. Sam was dismissed from his job and was left completely without resources. I heard at the time from the O'Kennedys of Lindsay Road that P. S. O'Hegarty, who was Secretary of the Post Office, told him to ignore the dismissal notice and come back to his job.[14]

Maguire refused to accept this proposal, and for the remainder of his life he lived with the O'Kennedy family. They supported him and provided him with all his requirements until a few months before his death. He went home to his family in Dunmanway to die.

T. J. Murphy, Labour Party TD for West Cork and a resident of Dunmanway, raised the dismissal of Maguire in the Dáil on 12 May 1926. He described Maguire's career in the UK post office and his return to work in Dublin. He said Maguire would attend a trial to investigate the charges against him. He then stated that the army mutiny had taken place in March 1924 and the government had been correct in the actions it had taken at the time of the mutiny, but Maguire was dismissed in December of that year. If he had been involved in the mutiny he should have been dismissed in March. If the government could afford to wait for eight months, his actions must not have been very serious.[15]

Murphy later said that Maguire was 'walking the streets of Dublin at the present time, sad to relate, practically penniless and absolutely broken up'. He pointed out that Maguire was a Protestant and that 'he might be excused for not giving the service that he gave to the country'. But all the time, because of the position he was in, he gave very considerable service and was one of the people who did a great deal in helping to set up the State.[16]

Murphy then referred to what might be regarded as a precedent for Maguire's case: many of the army officers who had been dismissed in 1924, following the mutiny, received their pensions, and some national teachers who had fought against the government in the Civil War were allowed to continue in their jobs. In the light of these facts, he pleaded for Maguire to be treated in a similar manner. He concluded:

> I repeat the appeal I made yesterday to the President that there are two aspects of this case that might be considered; one is that if there are charges made against this man he has not had an opportunity of answering them, and even if the Executive Council will not adopt the policy of putting this man in possession of the details of the charges made against him and even if they feel that there is a certain doubt as to whether he did things, surely they might have given him the benefit of the doubt, if they are to save his body in the grave from being a reproach to their administration.[17]

Two deputies, J. O'Doherty and T. MacCurtain, expressed support for T. J. Murphy's appeal. Deputy MacCurtain said he believed that when Maguire moved back to Dublin to work in the post office he brought part 'of his superannuation allowance, a sum of between £3,000 or £4,000'.[18] This contributory superannuation consisted of deferred pay and meant that Maguire had 'a reasonable expectation of a pension', but he had been dismissed without receiving one. By contrast, the army officers dismissed because of the army mutiny did receive pensions, even though the pension scheme under which they had been paid had been created after they were dismissed. Thus, by contrast with Maguire, they could have had no reasonable expectation of a pension. MacCurtain also urged the government to take into account the role that Maguire had played in the War of Independence.

Minister for Home Affairs Kevin O'Higgins replied that Maguire had not been dismissed because of involvement in the mutiny, even though it was 'beyond question this man was implicated, and deeply implicated, in those troubles'.[19] He continued by saying that Maguire's name had been reported in the newspapers in connection with the process of the return of weapons stolen from the National Army, and that 'He was a figure, a very prominent and authoritative figure, in that particular crisis, but the fact that he figured in that crisis, did not lead to his dismissal.'

O'Higgins stated that Maguire's dismissal had occurred in December because the government received definite information (although it refused to disclose its source) that there was an attempt to undertake another mutiny. This information suggested that those involved in this second attempt believed that the first mutiny had failed because it was confined to the officers in the army. For the second mutiny an attempt would be made to include soldiers who were not officers and, in particular, non-commissioned officers (NCOs – soldiers with the rank of sergeant and corporal) who were of pivotal importance in the army.

O'Higgins went on to say that in December 1924 twenty NCOs and men and two majors were dismissed, and two civil servants were dismissed, one of those being Mr Maguire. In reply to a question, he said the other civil servant was 'a man named Bolger'.

Then, in response to the question 'Did the Executive Council give Mr Maguire any chance of refuting these charges?', he replied that 'it was inadvisable, impossible in fact, to table evidence in support of that charge, because to table evidence would reveal the source, and to reveal the source would lead to casualties, and the Deputy knows it'. O'Higgins said the circumstances which justified the dismissal were very special as a group of men were 'talking and thinking in terms of assassination, in terms of a *coup d'état*, in terms of suborning the forces of the State, civil and military' – a situation that was similar to the earlier mutiny in 1924.

Turning to Maguire's case, he said that Maguire's health and twenty-six years of service were not relevant, because it would mean that a civil servant with many years of service would 'have immunity to do what he likes'. Because an ex-civil servant suffered from ill health, it would not be sufficient justification for his re-employment. Furthermore, if a man took a salary from the state, but then attempted to undermine the state, he must accept the inevitable consequence of his actions, and it would be ridiculous if the state were to find itself dismissing and then reinstating such men. He continued:

> I answer this matter this evening because I was presiding at the Executive Council when this dismissal took place ... I have now been a member of the Executive Council for some years and there were few decisions taken there regarding which I hold so firmly the conviction that they were right, and sound and necessary, as I do in the case of this particular decision. The accuracy of the information, the definiteness of the action taken on the information, saved the Army and the country from a recurrence of the troubles which had taken place in the early portion of that year. The accuracy of the information, the definiteness of the action taken on the information, discouraged any further attempts to suborn the uniformed servants of the State. The privates and the N.C.O.s before leaving the Curragh for their homes admitted the accuracy of the information. I am aware that the officers and the civil servants did not, but I then believed and I now believe in the accuracy of the information, and so believing, I believe in the justice of the action taken on it.[20]

6

DEATH

Sam Maguire died of tuberculosis on 6 February 1927, aged forty-nine, and was buried in the cemetery of St Mary's in Dunmanway. The *Irish Independent* reported:

> The funeral took place at his native Dunmanway of Mr Sam Maguire, who up to a year ago, was a well-known official of the GPO Customs department. He had 25 years of service in the GPO London, where he was a close friend of the late General Collins, with whom he was very intimately identified in the movement which led up to the rebellion. He held the rank of Lieutenant General in the Volunteers, and was director of intelligence in Great Britain during the Black and Tan period. He played a leading part in the transport of arms and ammunition to this country in pre-truce days.[1]

The following appeared in *The Southern Star*:

'Sam Maguire is dead' … it was clear to all who knew him that the end could not be far off … He had been in indifferent health for some time, but hopes were entertained that he would recover.

… his passing should be numbered amongst the 'Death of those who for their country die' as truly as if he had pined in prison facing the firing squad.

I made his acquaintance in the rooms of the Irish National Club, Chancery Lane, London … Of powerful athletic build, he was admittedly one of the foremost footballers of the period and captained the London-Irish combinations in successive All-Ireland finals; and at Dublin in 1906 was captain of the team which won the 'Boss Croker Cup'.

The early 1900s was the hey-day of the GAA activities in England … [this] was in no small measure due to Sam's efforts in roping in every newcomer to the 'big smoke'.

Many a boy-clerk will say 'well, my spiritual and temporal salvation can be traced to my meeting with Sam Maguire; if I had not been roped in to the GAA I would have swelled the "Legion of the Lost".'

… In the Anglo-Irish war he was one of General Collins' most trusted lieutenants, being delegated Intelligence Officer and charged with the acquisition of arms and equipment. In this connection he brought off some 'marvellous acquisitions' in raids and otherwise, and only in one instance – that in which young McInerney lost his life – was there any resultant casualty.[2]

In his oration at the graveside, J. J. Walsh said:

As a great Gael and an equally great patriot, Sam Maguire was unique in one respect in his generation. He was born of a minority that were, and still very largely remained, alienated in culture and outlook from the majority of their countrymen.

... But the fact that he stood out from his immediate surroundings in that respect would not in itself be a justification for the exceptional mark of respect which would henceforth mark his resting place. His subsequent services in the fight for freedom were the predominant determination. In that simple headstone it was written of him that from the beginning to the end of his career he gave all that one could give that his country might be free. Greater love than that was given to no man and equal to only a few.

... In London ... At once he threw himself into the work of Gaelic culture through the Gaelic League and the GAA, and because of his great energy, transparent honesty of purpose and natural ability, in a brief time he rose to the leadership of the Irish in the British metropolis.

... Above and beyond everything else in the world Sam Maguire ambitioned the day that the flag of a free nation would unfurl from the bastions of alien government. That was his sole and consuming hope, and the immensity of the role he played in subsequent years was the measure of his determination. Strange to relate little was known generally of the important activities of that great Gael. He preferred to leave the limelight to others.

At other times and by other men it was hoped that their true significance would find appropriate record. It was not unknown, however, that for many years he was head centre of the IRB in Britain, and it was of more than passing interest to recall that it was he who initiated that greatest of all guer-rilla warriors – General Michael Collins – in to the secrets of Fenianism; and if there had been one regret in his life it was the fact that illness had robbed him of the chance of associa-tion with that small army of Irishmen who crossed to Dublin to participate in the Rising of Easter Week.

But the years that ensued gave him ample compensation. During those years of stress and strain and working in a hos-tile relationship he was the channel by which every important and dangerous operation of the IRA in Britain was carried through. Not alone did he shoulder that heavy responsibi-lity, but it was worthy [to] record that through his immediate supervision passed large quantities of arms, ammunition and money on their way to Ireland from other lands. Truly the part he was called on to play in the struggle which history as-sociated with the terror of the Black and Tans must assuredly assure his name and fame to posterity …[3]

Walsh concluded by saying that Sam Maguire lived and died a great Irishman and patriot. That day the men and women of that town and district felt glad to pay to his memory all the respect in their power.

The people of Dunmanway continue to remember Sam Maguire and in 2017 installed 'The Sam Maguire Community Bells' in St Mary's Church, which will be used to keep the memory of Sam alive, to tell his story and the history of the town from where he came.

7

CREATION OF THE SAM MAGUIRE CUP

There were immediate moves on Sam Maguire's death at both national and local levels to commemorate him in some appropriate manner because of his work for the IRB and the GAA. Dan McAuliffe, who had worked with Maguire during the War of Independence in London, claimed that the first to suggest a memorial to Maguire was Jerome Hurley (IRA commandant from Dunmanway), who mentioned it to Ben O'Kennedy.[1] When Maguire had visited Dublin from London for consultation with Michael Collins, he had stayed with O'Kennedy, and also when he later lost his job.

Maguire's later career provided a difficulty for any official commemoration. He had taken the side of the Free State in 1922, which made him an opponent of the new anti-Treaty party, Fianna Fáil. But he had also been dismissed by the Free State government for attempting to start a mutiny in the army. This meant that neither Cumann na nGaedheal, the political party that was formed from the pro-Treaty section of Sinn Féin and was in government at this point, nor Fianna Fáil could claim him as a hero.

On 19 March 1927 the local news column 'Dunmanway Notes' in *The Southern Star* (written by the Dunmanway correspondent for the paper) reported that a memorial committee had been formed in Dublin and requested that donations should be sent to that committee. The committee members were:

President: Dr Mark Ryan [IRB member; also prominent in the London GAA and a member of the Hibernians GAA club].

Chairman: Dr Patrick McCartan [IRB member, TD in the early Dáils and stood for election as president of Ireland in 1945].

Vice-Chairmen: Frank Fahy TD; Patrick Belton TD; Michael Moloney [loyal and trusted courier between Sam and Michael Collins].

Trustees: James Kirwan; Thomas Moore [famous hurler, well-known publican and chairman of Faugh's GAA club for forty years].

Treasurers: B. O'Kennedy [friend of Sam Maguire]; J. Hurley [IRA commandant, Dunmanway, County Cork].

> Secretaries: Colonel S. Murphy; D. McAuliffe [IRB member and later a commandant in the Irish army].[2]

What is significant about the membership of the committee is that many of its members were very important figures in the IRA, GAA and Sinn Féin and also from commercial life in Dublin. Moreover, James Kirwan's pub had been an important venue during the War of Independence when it was frequently used for meetings by Michael Collins, Dan Breen and others.[3]

The committee's appeal began by quoting from Patrick Pearse's oration at the grave of Jeremiah O'Donovan Rossa at Glasnevin cemetery in Dublin in 1915 and then stated:

> Another great Gael from Rossa's gallant county [Cork] has now passed to his eternal reward. That Gael was Sam Maguire … What Pearse said of Sam's great prototype can with equal truth can be said of Sam Maguire, for indeed he was the quintessence of all that is great and noble in the cause of Irish nationality … The teachings of Tone [Wolfe Tone (1763–1798), regarded by later generations of Irish republicans as 'the father of Irish Republicanism'] and Emmet [Robert Emmet (1778–1803), whose famous speech from the dock during his trial for treason became an inspiration for later generations of radical republicans], personified in himself, were passed along to all with whom he came in contact.

A representative committee has been formed for the purpose of erecting a suitable Monument to his memory ... [and] now appeal for funds to the country as a whole, to his many friends in Ireland, Britain and America ... who during the Anglo-Irish war ... were destined to be in close touch with him. That he gave his services ... without gain or reward, that he gave his time, his energy and ability to the one object which dominated his mind – Ireland a nation, Ireland free ... is only typical of the great man he was and the great principles he exemplified.

To deal with his work in his half century of years in a short space would be impossible. The Irish Republican Brotherhood, the GAA (being chairman of the London County Board for a number of years as well as captaining London Irish football teams); the Gaelic League, and the Irish Self-Determination Movement abroad, absorbed every moment of his spare time.

He visioned Ireland as Patrick Pearse did when he said – 'Not free merely but Gaelic as well; not Gaelic merely but free as well'.

Sam Maguire gave thirty years of his life to the National cause, working seriously all the time, always confident in the hope that even in his lifetime the people of Ireland would at last be justified in writing the epitaph of Robert Emmet [who said his epitaph should not be written until Ireland was free]. He has gone to his grave without witnessing the realisation of his ideals. It is confidently hoped that the perpetuation of his countrymen will help to preserve the honour and integrity of his countrymen and that his services so freely given will not go unrecognised.[4]

The historical record is not clear, but it seems that in the year following his death there was an attempt to create a Sam Maguire memorial park in his native town of Dunmanway. The 'Dunmanway Notes' reported a year later:

Many of the old citizens and older generations of the Dohenys [local Gaelic football club] as well as the youthful ones who were enthusiastic over the proposed Town Park to be established in Dunmanway and which it was thought would be a perpetual memorial to the late lamented patriot, Mr Sam Maguire ... will be greatly saddened that the Memorial Park is not to be established in Dunmanway. The Dublin Committee have apparently altered their minds as to the form of the Maguire memorial ...[5]

The first mention of the Sam Maguire Cup came at the GAA central committee meeting on 3 December 1927. Eoghan Corry, in his *History of Gaelic Football*, states that a medal was no longer seen as a sufficient prize for twentieth-century players; a trophy that could be raised in triumph at the end of the match was also needed as the defining moment of victory.

Corry also suggests that: 'Presenting the cup to a winning captain was a ceremony that attracted as much attention as the match, the focus shifting to the trophy rather than the abstract concept of the victory.'[6] In particular, Corry mentions that newsreel footage of the presentation of the Football Association Cup (soccer) in 1927, which was shown in many cinemas in Ireland, may have created the idea that Gaelic football needed its own trophy.

The extract from the minutes of the meeting where the idea of a cup was first introduced reads as follows:

> O'Toole [Luke O'Toole, the general secretary] reported that Mr Moore, treasurer of the Sam Maguire Memorial Committee intimated that the memorial committee intended offering a cup to the Central Committee to be named as the Sam Maguire Perpetual Challenge Cup to be held by the winner of the All-Ireland football championship from year to year.[7]

At the time the cup cost £300. In today's terms that sum is equivalent to €20,000. The cup is modelled on the Ardagh Chalice, which was discovered in a *lios* or ringfort in the townland of Reerasta near the village of Ardagh, County Limerick, in September 1868 by two local men, Jimmy Quin and Paddy Flanagan, a labourer working for Quin. Mrs Quin, Paddy's mother, had rented the land from the local convent.

The Quin family sold the chalice to the Bishop of Limerick for £50, and he in turn sold it to the Royal Irish Academy for £500! Some 24 centimetres in diameter and nearly 18 centimetres high, the bowl of the chalice holds 1.4 litres. The cup, made from more than 250 main components, is silver alloyed with copper, and is decorated with gold filigree, multicoloured enamels, a large rock-crystal, amber and malachite.

The commission to make the Sam Maguire Cup was given to Hopkins and Hopkins, jewellers and watchmakers of O'Connell Bridge, Dublin. However, this company did not have the facilities for such a big job. Instead, Hopkins and Hopkins contracted the work to silversmith Matthew J. Staunton, who had his business in D'Olier Street, Dublin.

Maitiú Standun, Staunton's son, confirmed in a letter printed in a newspaper in October 2003 that his father had indeed made the original Sam Maguire Cup back in 1928. Matthew J. Staunton (1888–1966) came from a long line of silversmiths going back to the Huguenots, who brought their skills to Ireland in the 1600s. Matt, as his friends knew him, served his time under the renowned Dublin silversmith Edmond Johnson, who in 1921 had made the Liam MacCarthy Cup, which is awarded each year to the team that wins the All-Ireland Senior Hurling Championship.

The bowl of the Sam Maguire Cup was hand-beaten from a single flat piece of silver. Even though it is highly polished, multiple hammer marks are still visible, indicating the manufacturing process. Having outsourced the manufacturing of the cup, Hopkins and Hopkins still had their own initials 'H&H' stamped on it, as was common practice.

At the time, everyone in the Irish silver trade was aware that Staunton had made the cup, and he would continue to maintain it until his business closed in 1966. Among the people involved in this trade was John Doyle, a silver polisher and plater who served his time under Staunton from 1948 to 1955 and worked with him right up to 1966. Doyle and a fellow worker, Éamon Aspil, then formed their own company, Doyle and Aspil Silversmiths. Doyle and Aspil repaired and polished the cup periodically for as long as it remained in use by the GAA.

Kildare was the first county to win the Sam Maguire Cup – in 1928, having defeated Cavan 2–06 to 2–05. This is how the local Kildare paper reported the first presentation of the cup:

> A pleasant little ceremony followed the match when Willie Gannon, the Kildare Captain, was called to the Grand Stand and there presented by Dr McCartan, a close friend of the late Sam Maguire, with the … cup. …
>
> The cup is of very large dimensions and is a beautiful specimen of the silversmith's art. It commemorates the memory of

a noted Gael and great Irishman who was a main pillar of the Irish movement in England for many years. The cup is a perpetual one and will be held each year by the All-Ireland Senior Football Champions.[8]

The original trophy was retired in 1988; it had received some damage over the years as it had travelled around schools, clubs, pubs and, indeed, throughout the world. The GAA commissioned a replica from Kilkenny-based silversmith Desmond A. Byrne. The replica trophy, nicknamed 'Sam Óg', has been used ever since. Meath's Joe Cassells was the first recipient of 'Sam Óg': Meath have the distinction of being the last team to lift the old Sam Maguire and the first team to lift the new one, following their back-to-back victories against Cork in 1987 and 1988. In 2010 the GAA asked the same Kilkenny silversmith to produce another replica (the third Sam Maguire Cup), although this was to be used only for marketing purposes. The original Sam Maguire Cup is permanently on display in the GAA's museum at Croke Park.

In 1922 the London County Board had given the Liam MacCarthy hurling cup to the GAA to commemorate the chairperson of the board, Liam MacCarthy. Similarly in 1927, the board offered a cup for football, named after another chairperson of the board, Sam Maguire. However, when it became clear that the Dublin committee was attempting to do the same thing, London decided to retain their cup. The cup London retained became the All-Britain Junior Inter-County Championship cup. This competition is managed by the British Council of the Gaelic Athletic Association or British GAA, the only provincial council of the GAA outside Ireland, which is responsible for Gaelic games in Great Britain. The teams that compete for this Sam Maguire Cup include London, Manchester, Leeds, Birmingham, Scotland, Gloucestershire, Warwickshire, Herefordshire, Yorkshire, Hertfordshire and Lancashire. There are also third-level student clubs, including Dundee University, John Moores University in Liverpool and Saint Mary's University, London. The GAA counties cover wider areas than their names suggest: for example, the Hertfordshire County Board oversees clubs in Hertfordshire, Bedfordshire, Cambridgeshire and Oxfordshire; Gloucestershire GAA reaches into South Wales; Warwickshire GAA includes Staffordshire and Birmingham; and so on. The GAA continues to thrive in Britain, a fact of which Sam Maguire would no doubt be proud.

8

SIGNIFICANT MOMENTS IN THE HISTORY OF THE ALL-IRELAND FINALS

Kerry's First Sam Maguire Victory: 1929

During the 1920s, before the Sam Maguire Cup was first awarded in 1928, Kerry had won the competition twice, in 1924 and 1926. Following a double by Kildare in 1927 and 1928, Kerry won the cup for the first time in 1929, beating the reigning champions 1–08 to 1–05. This victory was the first win of Kerry's first four-in-a-row. They went on to beat Monaghan in 1930, Kildare again in 1931 and Mayo in 1932.

On the Friday before the 1930 final the legendary Dick Fitzgerald, who wrote the first coaching manual, *How to Play Gaelic Football*, died in an accident. There was a suggestion that out of respect for him the Kerry team should not play the match, but the decision was made to play as it was thought that winning the game would, in fact, be the best way to commemorate him. The Artane band played Chopin's funeral march before the match.

The First Acceptance Speech: 1933

The first recorded acceptance speech was given by the Cavan captain, Jim Smith, in 1933. It was described as 'a brief acceptance speech on how his life's ambition had been achieved'.[1] The result was Cavan 2–05, Galway 1–04.

Controversy in the Final: 1937

At the end of the game between Cavan and Kerry in 1937, Cavan scored a point which put them ahead by one point. However, the referee had already blown for a foul by a Cavan player, but due to the noise the whistle was not heard. The result was announced, over the public address and the radio, as a one-point win by Cavan. The correct result was established at a later time as a draw, 2–05 and 1–08. Sadly for Cavan, Kerry won the replay on a score of 4–04 to 1–07.

Micheál Ó hÉithir's First Broadcast: 1938

In May 1938 Micheál Ó hÉithir and four others did a five-minute test commentary during the National Football League game between Dublin and Louth at Croke Park. Dr T. J. Kiernan, Director of Broadcasting at Radio Éireann, was so impressed by Ó hÉithir's commentary that he asked the eighteen-year-old to do the commentary for the second half of the game. On 14 August Ó hÉithir made his first public broadcast, when he commentated on the All-Ireland football semi-final between Galway and Monaghan in Mullingar. Galway beat Monaghan 2–10 to 2–03.

A month later he made his first All-Ireland-final broadcast when he did the commentary on the drawn game between Galway and Kerry: Galway 3–03, Kerry 2–06. The match was replayed on Sunday 23 October 1938, when Galway won what was a very controversial game. A few minutes from the end the referee blew twice, first to award a free to Kerry and a second time because a Galway player was too close to the Kerry free-taker. Because it was so close to the end of the game and the whistle was blown twice, usually a signal for the end of the match, the Galway supporters interpreted it as the end of the game and came onto the pitch. Kerry supporters complained that the final whistle had gone too early and alleged that no extra time for stoppages had been played.

In the stand Taoiseach Éamon de Valera congratulated the Bishop of Galway. Then an announcement over the public-address system was made that the match was not, in fact, finished. Appeals to people to leave the pitch were eventually successful. Kerry fought back and scored a point, but it was too late, and at the official end of the match the score was Galway 2–04, Kerry 0–07. It was the first time Kerry had been beaten in a replay. The occasion was also the first time that a president of Ireland attended the final. Douglas Hyde, who had become the first president of Ireland in June 1938, following the introduction of the constitution in 1937, was present.

From 1938 until 1985 Ó hÉithir covered all the major GAA games in Ireland and abroad. Sadly, in 1985 illness ended his remarkable broadcasting career.

How the Ball from the 1944 Final was Saved

A 2006 newspaper interview with legendary Roscommon footballer Jimmy Murray revealed how the ball used in the 1944 final came close to being destroyed by burning:

> The football used in the 1944 All-Ireland final between Cavan and Roscommon hangs from a metal chain on the dark wooden ceiling in Jimmy Murray's pub in Knockcroghery … One night in 1990, a fire broke out in the pub, burning half the counter and destroying some of the All-Ireland photographs and memorabilia that Jimmy had placed around the room.
>
> The ball was suspended from a piece of string then, and in the heat it fell to the flames. A crowd had quickly gathered in the village trying to fight the fire, and one man dashed into

the melting room only to reappear, triumphantly shouting: 'I've got the ball. I've got the ball!'

'I said something like, "forget the ball and quench the bloody shop",' laughed Jimmy Murray during the week. 'But it would have been a shame if it had gone all right.'[2]

Jack Lynch: 1945 Final

For some Cork players there was a pleasing connection between Cork's All-Ireland victories in 1911 and 1945. The fathers of Éamonn Young and Derry Beckett – Jack Young and Jerry Beckett respectively – had been part of the victorious 1911 team, while their sons won All-Ireland medals with the 1945 team, when Cork defeated Cavan 2–05 to 0–07.

Derry Beckett joined an elite list of dual players who had won All-Ireland medals in both football and hurling. He had previously won an All-Ireland medal with the Cork hurling team in 1942. Paddy 'Hitler' Healy also joined this select group, winning an All-Ireland medal as a substitute to complement the winner's medal he claimed playing with the Cork hurlers in 1944. Cork's Jack Lynch, too, became a dual All-Ireland medallist. His achievement was the most spectacular of all: he had won four successive All-Ireland medals with the Cork senior hurling team between 1941 and 1944, and, by playing for the footballers, he became the first player to win five All-Ireland medals in succession.

Jack Lynch told the following amusing story about his journey to Croke Park on the day of the match. He had told the selection committee he would not meet the team at their hotel on Sunday morning, because he was living in digs in Rathgar and was on a bus route that ran to Croke Park. He found himself in a very long queue and saw several buses take only one or two people. In this situation, he felt he was justified in going to the head of the queue; the conductor, however, told him to go back to his position. Then Lynch showed him his football gear and told him he was due to play in the All-Ireland. The conductor agreed this gave him the right to jump the queue. When he arrived at Croke Park about fifteen minutes before the match, he knocked on the door of the Cork dressing room. The chairman of the selection committee answered the door, saying, 'Hello Jack Lynch, you were great to come.'[3]

The Antrim Objection: 1946 Semi-Final

Before the 1946 final there had been continuing controversy about the legitimacy of the hand pass in Gaelic football. A motion from Kerry to eliminate the hand pass at the 1945 congress did not receive the required two-thirds support (although it did get a majority), but later that year it was decided by the GAA authorities that the ball must be hit with the fist.

Leading up to the 1946 All-Ireland final, the successful use of the hand pass had been demonstrated by Antrim, who used it to win the Ulster Championship that year. The full-back for Kerry on the day of the semi-final, when they would meet the Ulster champions, was the towering and powerful army man Joe Keohane. Joe later became a selector on many Kerry teams and was one of Mick O'Dwyer's sideline mentors during the glorious era of the 1970s. Kerry adopted a tactic to cope with the hand passing by Antrim; this was to mark the man who would be receiving the pass, which meant rough tackling of the player. The crowd was not pleased but, diplomatically, Micheál Ó hÉithir did not mention it in his radio broadcast. Bill Casey of Kerry and Harry O'Neill of Antrim were both sent off.

The result was a Kerry victory: Kerry 2–07, Antrim 0–10. An account of the controversy reads:

> The Antrim officials were furious with the Kerry playing tactics and they formally protested to the Central Council and demanded that the result be overturned. However, the Antrim players were totally against the objection and their brilliant attacker Kevin Armstrong was quoted as saying, 'It was a mistake to protest, a regrettable mistake. The county board allowed themselves to be influenced by public opinion and I for one would not accuse Kerry of being over robust in that match.'[4]

Another account states:

> Antrim lodged a formal objection that the Kerry players were 'guilty of conduct calculated to bring the association into disrepute'.
>
> The Antrim County Board protested that 'members of the Kerry team continually indulged in rough play and repeatedly made deliberate and unwarranted assaults on our players during the progress of the match'.
>
> The Antrim board wanted Kerry thrown out of the championship, adding: 'The majority of these attacks, which resulted in serious injuries to many of our players, were made when they were not in possession of, or playing, the ball. Injuries, which we maintain were the result of deliberate attacks, were sustained by eight members of our team. We are prepared to submit evidence regarding the extent of their injuries.'
>
> ... The GAA Central Council met to consider the protest on the last Saturday in August and debated the issue for two hours before overruling the objection by 19 votes to 10. 'Antrim's advocates defeated their own case,' according to *The Kerryman*. 'Their autocratic bearing and dictatorial attitude roused the hostility of the southerners. The northerners were the self-appointed guardians of the association's honour. Its reputation was their only concern. They were charged with redeeming the good name of the GAA which the Kerry

rowdies had done so much to besmirch. All of which would be highly amusing if it were not so disgusting.'

Antrim produced nine medical certificates for their players. 'Nurtured in an atmosphere of religious intolerance and bitterness, the northern Gael has a very different mentality from his brother in the south,' *The Kerryman* noted. 'Thus we had the type of objection never heard previously in the 60-year history of the association.'[5]

The 1946 final was originally set for 22 September, but was delayed for two weeks as part of the 'Save the Harvest' campaign, which was due to the very bad weather that year. Kerry beat Roscommon in a replay of the final: Kerry 2–08 to Roscommon 0–10.

Final in New York: 1947

A very large number of Irish people lived in the USA in the early part of the twentieth century, and the GAA was present in many places in that country. During the Second World War (1939–1945), emigration from Ireland had fallen, and the GAA in the USA felt it needed a boost to revive interest in Gaelic football. A letter from an emigrant requesting that the All-Ireland be played in the USA was read to the GAA congress and the motion was passed. It later turned out that the letter was a forgery, but the decision was allowed to stand.

The year 1947 was also the hundredth anniversary of 'Black '47', the worst year of the Great Famine in Ireland.

Cavan and Kerry qualified for the final. The Cavan team travelled by air and the Kerry team by sea. Arriving first, Cavan had a longer period of collective training. The game was played in New York's Polo Grounds (home of the New York Giants baseball team) on Sunday 14 September. The fact that this was a baseball ground meant that it was smaller than a standard Gaelic football pitch.

The ball was thrown in by William O'Dwyer, mayor of New York. Kerry had a great start and were soon eight points ahead. The most controversial aspect of the game was that in the first half Kerry scored two goals that were disallowed, and the referee gave two free kicks. Kerry had a substantial lead in the early stages of the game and the Kerrymen later suggested that the referee did not want to see a one-sided result. Cavan replied that they stopped playing when they heard the referee's whistle and this allowed Kerry to score the goals.

In the second part of the first half, the Kerry player Eddie Downing was concussed when he hit the raised pitcher's mound. It had not been dismantled because it was the one used by the famous Babe Ruth early in his career – it would have been considered a kind of sacrilege to interfere with the mound. Kerry's Teddy O'Sullivan recalled:

The ground itself was like a car park, the field was 140 by 80 yards wide and because it was used for baseball there was the mound in the middle for the pitcher. We'd never seen anything like that before and we all thought this would have to be removed, but one of the Americans just gave us this stern look and said that it wasn't to be touched.[6]

Downing's injury was one of several.

By half-time Cavan had scored two goals and were leading by one point. They continued to dominate the second half and won on a final score of 2–11 to 2–07. Cavan's team members included John Joe O'Reilly, known as 'gallant John Joe', who captained the team. He died at the early age of thirty-four in 1952 due to a serious injury suffered playing football. The politician and government minister John Wilson was also a member of the team. Cavan player Peter Donohue scored eight points and was described in the New York newspapers as the 'Babe Ruth of Gaelic football'.[7]

The game was a great success, attracting an attendance of 34,941. Micheál Ó hÉithir did the radio commentary. The game began at 3 p.m. New York time, so the Irish audience heard the broadcast at 8 p.m. The link to Ireland via transatlantic cable had been booked for a few hours, but as the game started late and so ran beyond the closing deadline of 5 p.m., Ó hÉithir had to ask the firm providing the link on air to give him extra time to describe the final minutes of the game.[8]

The broadcast attracted a record-breaking audience. The newspapers reported that in Dublin groups of people gathered in restaurants and cafes to listen, and others listened outside the windows of houses in which the volume of the radio was turned up.

The 'Mayo Curse'

In 1950 and 1951 Mayo won the All-Ireland Football Championship twice in a row:

> 1950: Mayo 2–05, Louth 1–06
> 1951: Mayo 2–08, Meath 0–09

The Mayo team in these two finals included the legendary Seán Flanagan and Tommy Langan. In total eleven men were involved in both finals.

Mayo's lack of a win since then, despite a number of appearances in more recent finals, has led to the emergence of an old wives' tale that the failure to win since 1951 is due to a priest's curse. Apparently during a parade for the winners in Foxford, County Mayo, in 1951, the local priest became angry at the behaviour of the fans while a funeral was taking place. Moreover, he said that the players should have come down from the back of the truck parading them through the town, as a mark of respect to the dead.

In September 2013 a priest, Fr Padraic Costello of Foxford, where the original incident occurred, lifted the curse. He said that he had checked the parish records and could not find any reference to a funeral taking place on the day the curse is said to have been cast.

Despite this, Mayo's run of bad luck has continued and not only did they lose in 2013, after the curse was supposedly lifted, but they lost by a heartbreaking one point in the replay of the 2016 final. It has been suggested that the curse will not actually be lifted until all the members of the 1951 team have died!

'The Man in the Cap': 1949 and 1954

The 'man in the cap' refers to the Meath player Peter McDermott, a nickname given to him by Micheál Ó hÉithir. Peter had long hair, split in the middle and held down by use of a product like Brylcreem, and when he played, he wore a cap to keep his hair in place. It seems that it was quite common at the time for hurlers to wear a cap, but it was unusual for a footballer, so his wearing of this item of clothing attracted Ó hÉithir's attention. McDermott was a member of Meath's 1949 winning team and was also the referee for the 1953 final. In that match, there was a controversial penalty kick by

Armagh's Bill McCorry – the Armagh team claimed it was a goal, but McDermott decided the ball was wide. Kerry won that match by four points.

In 1954, at almost thirty-six years of age, when he was a member of the county board and a selector, McDermott was given the role of captain of the Meath team. Meath won the final against Kerry, making McDermott the only man to have refereed an All-Ireland final and played in a subsequent one.

McDermott was the organiser of the first football tour to Australia, in March 1968, and he was the manager of the Irish team for the games against Australia in 1984.

Hill 16: 1955 Final

It was during the 1955 final between Kerry and Dublin that Hill 16 (the railway-end terrace in Croke Park) became the main site for Dublin supporters.[9] It was long believed that the Hill's name came from the fact that it was constructed from rubble from O'Connell Street after the Easter Rising of 1916, although that is now known to be an urban myth.[10] During the 1955 game Tadhgie Lyne was the top scorer for Kerry, notching up six points. Kevin Heffernan played at full-forward for Dublin. The final score was Kerry 0–12, Dublin 1–6.

Polio Outbreak Delays Game: 1956 Final

In 1956 Cork qualified for both the football and hurling finals. However, in the summer of that year an epidemic of polio, a highly infectious disease, broke out in Cork and by August there were ninety cases in the city and thirty-four in the county. Both of the All-Ireland finals were delayed at the request of the Dublin health authorities as a result, as they were fearful of large numbers of Cork people possibly bringing the infection with them to Dublin.[11] When the games were finally played, on 23 September and 7 October respectively, the Cork team was defeated in both matches: the hurling result was Wexford 2–14, Cork 2–08; the football score was Galway 2–13, Cork 3–07. At the end of the hurling final, Christy Ring was shouldered off the field by the Wexford backs Bobby Rackard and Nicky O'Donnell – it was Ring's last final.

Mick O'Connell captains the Kerry Team: 1959 Final

Mick O'Connell was just twenty-two years old when he was captain of the Kerry team that beat Galway on a score of 3–07 to 1–04 in the 1959 All-Ireland football final. He was given his role because the divisional team South Kerry had won the county final in the previous year, which gave them the right to nominate the captain for the All-Ireland team. O'Connell was the only player from the divisional champions, Valentia, on the

South Kerry team. However, he did not think that the role was particularly significant in Gaelic football, stating that the captain's main purpose was to accept the cup if the team won.

O'Connell's speciality was high fielding; with only a few steps in his run he could rise higher than most players. In his autobiography, *A Kerry Footballer*, he stated:

> I practised several self-devised exercises to improve agility and pliability. One was to simulate the block down first on one side and then quickly across to the other side. This twisting and turning, when continued on for a while, was a great workout for the midriff section. Hurdling rows of wire fencing, approximately three feet high, which were dividing the field next to where I trained, was another exercise that I relied a lot on. Allowing myself only a very short run-up, I repeated this jump rapidly over and back several times. This served the purpose of strengthening the jumping muscles.[12]

According to O'Connell's long-time midfield partner, the late Seamus Murphy, on one occasion: 'I was waiting under a dropping ball with Phil Stuart of Derry when I caught a glimpse of a pair of knees above my shoulder and hands gripping the ball. It was Mick O'Connell.'[13]

O'Connell also had a very close relationship on the field with Mick O'Dwyer. Brendan O'Sullivan wrote of this:

Later in his career he had a telepathic understanding with corner forward, Mick O'Dwyer. O'Connell would gather the ball in the centre of the field, O'Dwyer make a run towards the goal, O'Connell kick the ball towards the corner flag. O'Dwyer double back, having sent his marker the wrong way, collect the pass and slot it over the bar.[14]

O'Connell lived on Valentia Island and would row to the mainland on the day of the match; he would return on the same day, even if it meant rowing in the dark. He accepted the cup in 1959, but he returned home to the island on the night of the match – he did not stay to celebrate with his teammates in Dublin.

The Nine All-Ireland Football Finals contested by Mick O'Connell:

Won 4, lost 5

1959: Kerry 3–07, Galway 1–04

1960: Down 2–10, Kerry 0–08

1962: Kerry 1–12, Roscommon 1–06

1964: Galway 0–15, Kerry 0–10

1965: Galway 0–12, Kerry 0–09

1968: Down 2–12, Kerry 1–13

1969: Kerry 0–10, Offaly 0–07

1970: Kerry 2–19, Meath 0–18

1972: Offaly 1–13, Kerry 1–13; replay: Offaly 1–19, Kerry 0–13

Kerry v Down: 1960 Final

The teams in the 1960 final were Kerry and Down, meeting for the first time. Kerry, the champions of the previous year, were expected to win. However, they lost; the final score was Down 2–10, Kerry 0–08. This was a highly significant marker in the history of All-Ireland football, as it was the first ever victory by a Northern Irish team. According to Dónal McAnallen:

> While the GAA was proud not to recognise the north–south border in any of its internal matters, it was viewed as a special feat to take the Sam Maguire Cup north of the border for the first time. For many northern nationalists, these feats proved that they were not doomed to subjection in their lives.[15]

Down's success was the result of a carefully planned development programme, which was based on the style of play developed by Dublin in the 1950s. Dublin football at that time was primarily driven by the St Vincent's club, who developed their players through school leagues, creating a very slick, 'city-type' style of football.[16] The Down team included the McCartan brothers, Joe Lennon and Seán O'Neill. James McCartan scored a goal early in the second half, when the score was drawn. Later in the half, Paddy Doherty beat Kerry goalkeeper Johnny Culloty with a penalty kick.

The attendance of 87,768 at the game was the largest of any up to that date. When, in 1961, Down won a second All-Ireland, beating Offaly by 3–06 to 2–08, that game also recorded a large attendance: 90,556 spectators.

First Televised Final and Fastest Goal: 1962

The precursor of today's RTÉ television, Telefís Éireann, began broadcasting on 31 December 1961. The organisation was very interested in broadcasting Gaelic games, but the GAA was worried that televising games would reduce attendance at the matches. So, in 1962 coverage was limited to the All-Ireland hurling and football finals, the two All-Ireland football semi-finals and the two Railway Cup finals (in 1927 the Great Southern and Western railway company had donated a cup to be known as the Railway Cup, played for in an interprovincial competition in both football and hurling). The first time that Gaelic games were seen on Irish television was on 17 March 1962, when Telefís Éireann carried live coverage of the Railway Cup hurling final between Leinster and Munster. Leinster won 1–11 to 1–09.

The televised 1962 All-Ireland football final saw Kerry beat Roscommon 1–12 to 1–06. The match also featured the fastest goal ever scored in a final. Garry McMahon of Kerry scored after just thirty-four seconds. In *In Praise of Football*, Gabriel Fitzmaurice describes how the parish priest in

Shanagolden, County Limerick, set up a TV set in the parish hall and charged an attendance fee for those who wished to see the game. He attracted a very large audience – people in West Limerick were passionate about Gaelic football.[17]

On 5 September 1971 history would be made again, when Tipperary's defeat of Kilkenny (5–17 to 5–14) in the All-Ireland hurling final was the first Gaelic game to be televised in colour.

Galway's Three-in-a-Row: 1964, 1965 and 1966

Galway won the final in 1964, 1965 and 1966. The previous time this had been achieved was by Kerry, when they won three in a row in 1939, 1940 and 1941.

In 1964 Galway won by five points, 0–15 to Kerry's 0–10. After John Donnellan had accepted the cup, he was told that his father Mick had died while watching the game in the stand. Michael (Mick) Donnellan had founded a political party, Clann na Talmhan, in 1939, to represent the interests of the small farmers in the west of Ireland; he was a representative of the party in the Dáil from 1943 to his death. Clann na Talmhan asked John to stand in the election for the vacancy left by his father. He did stand for election, but as a Fine Gael candidate, and won the seat, making him a serving TD when he played in the All-Ireland finals in 1965 and 1966.

In 1965 Galway won by 0–12 to Kerry's 0–9. Three players were sent off: John Donnellan and, from the Kerry team, two brothers: Derry and John (Thorny) O'Shea.

In 1966 Galway's score was 1–10 to Meath's 0–07.

Galway's team remained largely unchanged for the three finals, with eleven of their players taking part in all three. Galway goalkeeper Johnny Geraghty was one, and he did not concede a goal in any of the games. He is still regarded as one of the best ever goalkeepers in the game and, as such, attracted attention from soccer clubs in England. Before the 1960s the goalkeeper, like outfield players, could not touch the ball on the ground. When this rule was changed, Geraghty introduced soccer-style diving saves. Because of his agility he was nicknamed 'the cat' – for the style of his saves and his ability to rise high enough to fist the ball over both backs and forwards. In that period outfield players were given more opportunity to play in 'the square', the small rectangle in front of the goal – in modern times outfield players cannot be in 'the square' before the ball arrives in that part of the pitch – and there was very little protection for the goalkeeper from opposing forwards.

'A rally which for grit and guts and spirit surpassed anything': 1967 Final

The 'man in the cap', Peter McDermott, was the coach of

the Meath team that played Cork in the 1967 final. Meath scored only one point in the first half, while Cork scored three points. However, the Meath that emerged in the second half were a very different team. In his *Irish Times* column, Paddy Downey wrote: 'Their second half transformation was so unexpected that it seems incredible. Nevertheless it was a rally which for grit and guts and spirit surpassed anything I have seen in a final.'[18]

Cork were denied a goal late in the second half when the referee decided that Con Paddy O'Sullivan's pass to Flor Hayes was too short. The final score was Meath 1–09, Cork 0–09.

Down Maintain an Unbeaten Record: 1968 Final

In the 1968 final Down once again faced Kerry. Two members of each side had played in the 1960 final: Mick O'Connell and Mick O'Dwyer for Kerry and Down's Seán O'Neill and Paddy Doherty. Six minutes into the match, O'Neill scored a goal, and a short time later John Murphy scored a second goal for Down. Late in the game Kerryman Brendan Lynch, playing in his first All-Ireland, scored a goal from a free, but, despite this, Down hung on and maintained their unbeaten record against the Kingdom on a final score of 2–12 to Kerry's 1–13.

Kerry Wear the Blue of Munster: 1969 Final

In the 1969 final, because the competing teams Kerry and Offaly both used green and gold, it was decided that Kerry would wear the blue of Munster for the match.

In advance of the match, according to Eoghan Corry, there was some doubt over whether the great Mick O'Connell, who had led the Kerry team to victory in 1959, would play: 'The team entered the field without him, wearing the blue jerseys of Munster, and then, to a huge roar, O'Connell appeared wearing his own personal blue jersey.'[19]

Johnny Culloty had taken up the position of goalkeeper for Kerry following a cartilage operation that prevented him from playing in his usual position as a forward. A notable feature of the game were the three amazing saves he made. Although it was a disappointing match overall, Paddy Downey wrote in his *Irish Times* column:

> There were however a few redeeming features in the game. The most admirable of these was DJ Crowley's magnificent midfield performance for Kerry. This, surely, was the finest game of the Rathmore man's career. With Mick O'Connell playing below his usual brilliant form, Crowley took on more work than would normally be required of him at midfield and despite a couple of hard knocks he dominated the game from start to finish.[20]

First Eighty-Minute Final: 1970

At the GAA congress in 1969, it was decided that the duration of the final would be increased from sixty to eighty minutes for the first time in 1970. It has been suggested that this decision was taken to provide the same 'value for money' as soccer (ninety minutes of play) and rugby (eighty minutes of play) provided. Other changes that may have encouraged or, at the very least, helped with this increase in game time was that the football was now covered with plastic, which meant it would not become soggy and difficult to play in wet weather, and players' boots were also lighter than was earlier the case, which would have been less tiring on the legs.

In the 1970 final, Kerry v Meath, Den Joe Crowley of Kerry scored what has been described as 'the goal of the century' four minutes from the end.[21] Following a solo run from the middle of the field, Crowley burst through the Meath defence to put the ball in the back of the net.[22] The main point of interest for spectators during the game was how the 'traditional' style of football of Kerry would fare against the 'modern' and 'scientific' approach of Meath, but Kerry won by 2–19 to Meath's 0–18. The Kerry manager, Jackie Lyne, said afterwards that this was 'our answer to the Gormanston [Meath team's training ground] Professors and their blackboard tactics'.[23]

The Birth of 'Heffo's Army': 1974 Final

Dublin had last won an All-Ireland in 1963 and were not in good shape in 1974. The county had been relegated to division two of the National League in 1973 and had not won a first-round match in Leinster for three years.

The re-emergence of Dublin as a significant Gaelic football power began with the decision to choose Kevin Heffernan as the manager of the Dublin team in 1973. The need for change was emphasised by the fact that the 1973 team included players who had been defeated by Longford in the recent past. The new manager introduced a very strict training regime and also developed an innovative emphasis on switching tactics to negate the strengths of opposing teams.

On 19 May 1974 Dublin was due to meet Wexford in the Leinster semi-final. Two days before the game, bombs exploded in Dublin and Monaghan. Due to this attack the match was postponed for a week. Because both teams were held in such low esteem, the game was to be played before the National Football League final between Kerry and Roscommon, and little or no concern was created by the change. Dublin beat Wexford by 3–09 to 0–06. This game was so insignificant that *The Irish Times* did not even have a staff reporter at the game. Another report suggests that some of the spectators who were waiting for the league final actually laughed at Dublin's performance.[24]

Dublin beat Meath in the Leinster final, but were not expected to beat the reigning champions, Cork, in the All-Ireland semi-final. There was a rumour that Cork had already booked a hotel for the weekend of the final. Despite this, Dublin achieved an impressive victory. At the midway point in the second half of the game, Cork had sixteen men on the field. Martin Doherty had been sent on to replace Ned Kirby, but Kirby, unaware that he had been substituted, remained on the pitch and the referee failed to notice the extra man. Kevin Heffernan went onto the pitch to drag him off, but Kirby refused to leave and stayed in the game. Despite the extra man and a penalty scored by Jimmy Barry-Murphy, Dublin won the semi-final 2–11 to Cork's 1–08.[25]

In the final, Galway led Dublin by 1–04 to 0–05 at half-time, but Dublin outscored them in the second half by 0–09 to 0–02. A crucial point in the second half was the award of a penalty to Galway. Liam Sammon had a very good kick, but Paddy Cullen made an amazing save. Dublin won the final by 0–14 to Galway's 1–06. When the game ended the Dublin fans invaded the pitch and raised a chorus of 'We want Heffo': it was the birth of 'Heffo's army'.

Curiously, in the programme for the game, the Dublin colours are listed as 'Blue and White', but in fact Dublin changed their strip to navy and blue at the start of the 1974 Championship.[26]

The success of the 1974 team led to a huge growth in the number of Dubliners attending Dublin games. The joke at the time was that many of them would need directions for how to get to Croke Park.

The Great Kerry–Dublin Rivalry: 1975 Final and Beyond

In April 1975, following the team's thirteen-point defeat by Meath in the National League quarter-final, Mick O'Dwyer was asked to take on the job of manager of the Kerry team. In its first season, O'Dwyer's young team would go on to outwit and outplay the champions, Dublin, in very poor conditions in the All-Ireland final. 1975 saw the final reduced from eighty minutes to seventy minutes and it also heralded the beginning of the great Kerry and Dublin rivalry.

In his autobiography O'Dwyer wrote:

> We trained like no team ever trained before. It was crazy stuff but they were young enough to take it and, anyway, I believed it was necessary because Dublin had raised the fitness bar … Had I kept the older lads on the panel they would not have been able for the training, and even if they were they would probably have revolted.[27]

The youngest players on the Kerry team, Pat Spillane and

Denis (Ogie) Moran, were both under twenty on the day of the final. The training regime involved six nights each week for several months. Considering that some players had to travel 190 kilometres to get to and from training, it required a serious commitment from them.

In the All-Ireland final Kerry's John Egan scored a goal after just three minutes, which boded well for the outcome and must have boosted the team's morale. However, the game was not without its problems for the Kingdom. In the twenty-third minute Michael (Mickey Ned) O'Sullivan, the Kerry captain, suffered a concussion as he tried to break through the Dublin defence. He was transferred to hospital and did not regain consciousness until 5.25 p.m., twenty-five minutes after the match had ended. When he woke up, he asked a nurse who had won the match. The result had been Kerry 2–12, Dublin 0–11.

Unusually, on the night of the match, many violent incidents put a great strain on the gardaí and the fire brigade. In one incident two men were stabbed in a match-related fight in a pub in Balgriffin, and the newspapers reported that a hundred people were injured.[28] It was not a common occurrence for such violence to manifest itself after a GAA match.

The unexpected win by Kerry in 1975 led commentators to suggest they would be the dominant team in the following

Two stabbed, 100 injured in after-match brawls

MICHAEL O'SULLIVAN captained the Kerry team which won yesterday's All-Ireland senior football final — but he did not know which team had won until 45 minutes after the game had finished.

For Michael, a 23-year-old physical education teacher from Kenmare, was knocked out in the 20th minute of the match as he tried to "waltz" his way through the Dublin defence.

He was carried off on a stretcher and rushed, still unconscious, by ambulance to Dublin's St. Laurence Hospital.

Following an X-ray he was transferred to Ward 3, where he did not regain full consciousness until about 5.25 — 45 minutes after the game had finished.

But the Kerry glory turned sour in Dublin last night when at least 100 people were taken to hospitals during after-match celebrations.

Ambulances were on almost constant call up to "closing time" ferrying injured people to hospital.

Said a harrassed fire brigade officer: "We have never been so busy. At least one hundred people have already been taken to hospital with injuries."

Two men were stabbed in a pub row at Balgriffen and were rushed to St. Laurence's Hospital, where information on their condition was not immediately available.

Gardai in Coolock, who were last night questioning two men in connection with the stabbing, said it appeared the incident occurred because of a row over the football final.

Last night the entire victorious Kerry team went to the hospital to see Michael.

Afterwards he said: "I lost my sight and memory completely for a while," he said. "I remember nothing after being tackled until I woke up in this hospital bed.

"But when my memory returned, the first thing I asked a nurse was 'Who won?' When I heard the news it was really fabulous and I shouted: 'That's great'."

Asked about the incident in which he was fouled, he said: "I don't remember very much about it. But I don't think anyone set out deliberately to injure me."

Meanwhile in Kenmare last night a new shelf was being cleared in Neddy Ned's where the Sam Maguire Cup will adorn the little pub on the Square, where the Kerry captain lives with his widowed mother. "I don't know where it will sit with all Michael's other trophies, but it must have pride of place," said his proud mother last night.

Mrs. O'Sullivan, who was pulling pints and accepting congratulations with equal graciousness, said she was terrified when she saw the stretchers brought on

(See Pages 11, 12 and 13)

Report from the *Irish Independent* of 29 September 1975 on the violence that followed the 1975 final.

years. However, in the 1976 All-Ireland final the tide turned and three goals from Brian Mullins, John McCarthy and Jimmy Keaveney gave Dublin a victory. The result (Dublin 3–08, Kerry 0–10) was Dublin's first victory over Kerry since the Sam Maguire Cup had first been presented. Kevin Heffernan's comment on Dublin's win was: 'I've waited twenty years for this.'[29] As a player in 1955, Heffernan had been on the Dublin team that was beaten by Kerry in the All-Ireland final.

Mick O'Dwyer was subsequently of the opinion that the 1975 victory may have gone to the heads of some of the young players. The result, in his opinion, was that they were less committed to training in 1976, and this may have been compounded by an easy semi-final win over Derry (Kerry 5–14, Derry 1–10). Moreover, the 1976 team also had injury worries. A few days before the match, seven of the team were not fit enough to train; some of them lined out even though they were not fully fit. Specifically, Jimmy Deenihan and Ger O'Keeffe both played, despite suffering from ankle injuries.

The growing rivalry can be seen in the attendance of 54,974 at the 1977 All-Ireland semi-final between the two teams, the largest crowd at an All-Ireland semi-final since 1962, when 60,396 had watched the same teams in action. In fact, it is likely that this game had a record audience, as it was also shown live on television.

The *Irish Independent* GAA correspondent Martin Breheny has listed this game as number one in the top ten of games that he has seen, and it is often considered to be one of the greatest games ever played. James McMahon described the game:

> Kerry were a goal to the good at the break – their green flag coming from Seán Walsh [when a goal is scored the umpire raises a green flag to validate the score and tell the

referee who should record the score] – in a period where the victors hit eight wides. However, it was Dublin's dominance of midfield in the second period and Bernard Brogan's introduction in that sector, that saw Heffo's men gain a real foothold. John McCarthy goaled shortly after the break to bring the sides level. Points were exchanged thereafter as the intensity level ratcheted up. Yet, it was the Dubs' graph that was rising faster.

In a move started by Brian Mullins, the ball eventually found its way to Tony Hanahoe, who slipped it off to David Hickey and the latter shot brilliantly to the back of the net for Dublin's second goal. Goal number three saw Hickey, Hanahoe and Bobby Doyle combine to set up Bernard Brogan for the clinching score as Dublin ran out five-point winners. They would go on to win a third All-Ireland in four years by beating Armagh in the decider.[30]

Mitchell Cogley wrote of it:

'Dublin are Magic; Kerry are Tragic.' This was one of the more flamboyant banners flourished before, during, and after Sunday's football semi-final at Croke Park; and it was only half right. There was nothing tragic about Kerry's display, but an exhibition of football that would easily have accounted for most teams and almost did it against Dublin until the champions unleashed a sustained spell of sheer magnificence which produced as blinding a display of football magic in the last ten minutes or so as I have ever had the exhilaration of seeing. What had gone before in the second half was enough to have rated the game close to epic quality and both teams very close to the best their counties have produced. But I doubt if I have ever seen, even from the great Kerry, Dublin, Galway, Cavan and Down teams, a closing spell like Dublin's this time, when all the latent talents jelled into a unit of excellence to which even this fine Kerry team had no answer.[31]

Dublin won convincingly by 3–12 to 1–13.

The following year both teams made it to the final, but this was to see a reverse in fortunes. A report described the battle to win the 1978 match in this way:

'BOYS THERE is a divorce, Sam is going south tonight.' The words were spoken by a big, cautious Kerryman at yesterday's All-Ireland Football Final at Croke Park, when Kerry had gone into a 15-point lead. He was referring, of course, to the Sam Maguire Cup, the All-Ireland trophy. But it was only at that stage, when Kerry had gone into a monumental lead that he even dared to suggest that the mighty Dublin had fallen.

Dublin fell with an almighty crash that even the Kerry people could not understand. For the record, the final score was Kerry 5–11; Dublin 0–9. It was a sad, sad occasion, and there was little triumphalism from the Kerry supporters. The winning margin perhaps was too great. The Dubs were silent. They carried their tattered banners with the pictures of their heroes away from Croke Park and only a few of them dared to raise their voices in song. The Kerry people sang about Kerry Long Ago and The Rose of Tralee, but clearly they would have loved a contest. There was no contest in Croke Park. It was dull and bad tempered.[32]

This All-Ireland final was Eoin (Bomber) Liston's first, and he scored three goals. The game is also remembered for a lob of the ball over Dublin goalkeeper Paddy Cullen's head into the goal by Mikey Sheehy. Cullen had had an early run-in with Ger Power and they clashed again three minutes before half-time. Referee Seamus Aldridge blew his whistle and the Dublin players assumed it would be a free out (a free kick). Cullen left his goal line to prepare to take the free. He even said to the referee that it must be a free out, although the latter did not respond. When Dubliner Robbie Kelleher handed the ball to Mikey Sheehy to take the free, Sheehy scored while Paddy Cullen was desperately backtracking to his goal.

The great Con Houlihan, in his column in *The Irish Press*, described this incident:

Its run-up began with a free from John O'Keeffe, deep in his own territory. Jack O'Shea made a flying catch and drove a long ball towards the middle of the 21-yard line.

M. Sheehy's fist put it behind the backs, breaking along the ground out towards Kerry's right. This time Paddy Cullen was better positioned and comfortably played the ball with his feet away from Sheehy.

He had an abundance of time and space in which to lift and clear but his pick-up was a dubious one and the referee Seamus Aldridge, decided against him. Or maybe he deemed his meeting with Ger Power illegal.

Whatever the reason, Paddy put on a show of righteous indignation that would get him a card from Equity, throwing up his hands to heaven as the referee kept pointing towards goal.

And while all this was going, M. Sheehy was running up to take the kick – and suddenly Paddy dashed back towards his goal like a woman who smells a cake burning.

The ball won the race and it curled inside the near post as Paddy crashed into the outside of the net and lay against it like a fireman who had returned to find his station ablaze.

Sometime, Noel Pearson might make a musical of this amazing final and as the green flag goes up for that crazy goal he will have a banshee's voice crooning: 'And that was the end of poor Molly Malone'. So it was. A few minutes later came the tea-break. Kerry went in to a frenzy of green and gold and a tumult of acclaim. The champions looked like men who had worked hard and seen their savings plundered by bandits. The great train robbers were out on the field for Act Two.[33]

The final score of Kerry 5–11, Dublin 0–09 produced a winning margin of seventeen points, one of the largest ever in a final.

Reunion

In a postscript to this story Dublin's Paddy Cullen and Robbie Kelleher were reunited with their nemeses Ger Power and Mikey Sheehy at a dinner hosted by the Austin Stacks club in Tralee on 25 February 2017. One of the highlights of the evening was the conversation concerning the infamous goal. When Paddy Cullen had a bar in Ballsbridge, he had photos of the goal on the wall. On one occasion when Sheehy was in the bar they were looking at the photos and Paddy said, 'Mikey, I made you famous.' Sheehy's answer to that was: 'Paddy, I made you rich!'

Robbie Kelleher also had a story to tell. He recalled an occasion when he was playing a game of golf in Clare. A man approached him and asked, 'Are you Robbie Kelleher, the Dublin footballer?', adding 'Jeez, it's great to meet a legend like you.' But then came the kicker. The man paused and said, 'You're the man who handed the ball to Mikey Sheehy aren't you?' On his return home that night, Kelleher told his wife that he wants 'The Man Who Handed The Ball To Mikey Sheehy' to be engraved on his tombstone.[34]

Five in a Row?: the 1982 Final

The 1982 final saw Kerry's attempt to win five in a row. The level of confidence in a Kerry victory against co-finalists Offaly was so high that a group named Galleon wrote a song to celebrate the five in a row.

The song's writer, Declan Lynch, recalls:

> The song was literally five years in the making. In 1978 a verse or two were written and sung in the pubs after the game. As Kerry proceeded to win 1979, 1980, 1981, further verses were written and sung in the celebrations after the games and Sam was going back to Kerry.
>
> So when 1982 came history beckoned. One more game. One more verse. But history and Seamus Darby had their own glorious way of letting us know that the record for our beloved Kerry would be set well and truly crooked. That Offaly have not won it since is irrelevant. There were players in their 1982 team who richly deserved to go home with Sam.[35]

The song was due for release the day after the final. The lyrics included:

Five in a row
Five in a row
I can't believe
We've got five in a row
They came from the north,
South, east and west
But to Micko's machine
They're all second best.

The group spent £5,000 to launch the single, and it was a hit. On the day before the match, the employees in a record-pressing factory were asked to work during the weekend to produce copies of the song. It was anticipated that sales would soar on Monday when Kerry would have won the final. At the same time T-shirts and sweatshirts with the logo 'Kerry 1982 5 in a row year' were on sale on the day of the final.[36]

Traditionally when Kerry brought the cup home the team would spend the first night, Monday, in Killarney and the second night in Tralee. In anticipation of the five in a row, the GAA in Tralee suggested that Tralee should be first, probably because so many of the players came from Tralee's Austin Stacks club.

A famous story told by the Offaly manager, Eugene Mc-Gee, related how in the week before the match he was very worried that Kerry would put Ogie Moran at full-forward. In that position Ogie would be marked by Offaly's usual full-back, Seán Lowry, and McGee felt Lowry would not be able to deal with Moran. But if Moran was selected in the corner, he believed Pat Fitzgerald would have the necessary speed against Moran, and Seán Lowry would be able to handle the likely alternative, Pat Spillane, as he would have the strength and guile to deal with Spillane. Moran had played in the corner in the defeats by Dublin in the All-Ireland in 1976 and the semi-final in 1977. Driving home from training, McGee was listening to the radio as the Kerry team was announced, and when Ogie Moran was selected at corner-forward he was ecstatic. He stopped the car, got out and punched the air.

On the Kerry side, the team had an informal sponsorship agreement with Adidas. At that time sponsorship was not officially recognised by the GAA. In 1982 there was a colour clash (both teams wore green and gold) and Adidas took the opportunity to provide Kerry with a new jersey (mint green with gold stripes). Adidas gear was produced by McCarters of Buncrana, Donegal, in a franchise arrangement. The Kerry team and management were happy with the jersey, but the GAA, at national level, was not. On the Friday before the match, Croke Park told the Kerry team they could not wear the new jersey. An urgent request was sent to McCarters. They managed a rush job and the original jerseys were delivered to the Kerry team's hotel late on Saturday night.

On the morning of the match the horoscope for Eugene

McGee's star sign in the *Sunday World* offered this prediction: if football is your game you will be successful.[37] Despite this, Kerry were four points ahead with just six minutes left to play. Mick O'Dwyer, in his autobiography, says that in such situations the referee tends to give the benefit of the doubt to the team that is behind. Offaly scored from frees and brought Kerry's lead back to two points and Kerry retreated into defensive mode to defend their lead.

At this point Seamus Darby replaced John Guinan on the Offaly team. Darby took up the corner-forward position and Kerry's wing-back Tommy Doyle followed him. This move meant that Kerry's wing-back had switched places with the corner-back. Darby received a pass from Liam O'Connor; Tommy Doyle jumped for the ball and Darby appeared to nudge him in the back. Doyle fell, and Darby scored one of the most famous goals in Gaelic football history. Darby later denied that he interfered with Doyle. In *Kings of September* he is quoted as saying, 'I held him, and as I took the ball I arsed him out of it.' Mick O'Dwyer's response was that if there was no interference, why would a player of Doyle's quality fail to judge the flight of the ball in such a way that he did not touch the ball and it fell into Darby's hands?[38] The referee said that Darby pushed out his backside and Doyle backed in to him. He did not see Darby's hands on Doyle, and this was confirmed by his umpires.

The final score was Offaly 1–15, Kerry 0–17.

The Twelve Apostles: 1983

The 1983 All-Ireland final (Dublin v Galway) saw some serious crowd control issues that almost led to tragedy. Up to this time there was overcrowding on both terraces, as it was possible to pay in at the entrances to the terraces in Croke Park. However, during this final a number of near fatal incidents occurred because of the crush on Hill 16, prompting a total redevelopment of the stadium to make it more modern and safer. The Hill was redeveloped as part of the refurbishment and the new Dineen Hill 16 terrace was officially opened in 2005.

In the 1983 Munster final, Cork had been surprise winners against Kerry, which meant that the 1983 All-Ireland final was the first since 1977 in which Kerry did not play. Cork's winning streak did not last, however, and they were beaten by Dublin in an All-Ireland semi-final replay in Cork.

The presence of Brian Mullins in the Dublin team on the day of the final was, literally, a miracle, as on 27 June 1980 he had lost control of his car on the Clontarf Road in Dublin and crashed into a lamp post. Seat belts were not compulsory at that time and Mullins did not like wearing one. This allowed him to throw himself out of the driver's seat; he said that this saved his life, because the seat belt would have put him at the point of impact. He ended up on the back seat. Even then, his injuries were severe and included a broken femur, broken cheekbones, lost teeth and a crack in the roof of his mouth. Following treatment, Brian could hardly walk without callipers or crutches for a year and was left with a noticeable limp. However, to the amazement and delight of his teammates he returned to play in the Leinster semi-final against Kildare in 1982.[39]

The conditions for the 1983 All-Ireland final were very poor, with rain and gale-force winds; many of the players blamed the conditions for the controversial incidents that took place during the game. From the start of play, players were slipping and colliding with each other. Because it was a final, the men were fully committed to winning the ball and this led to some serious clashes. The referee, John Gough from Antrim, said:

> It was the sort of day you don't want on All-Ireland final day. The weather determines how a game is going to turn out. That day the mixture of a very strong wind and rain meant the ball holding in the air, players getting underneath lots of players, slippery surface and all the rest.[40]

The first controversial incident was a Dublin goal in the eleventh minute. The Dublin manager, Kevin Heffernan, was treating an injured Joe McNally in the Galway square (the rectangle in front of the goal). McNally had begun his career as sub goalkeeper for Dublin, but had been rebooted as an outfield player by Heffernan.

The Galway goalie, Pádraig Coyne, had a poor kick-out due to the bad ground conditions; it went to Barney Rock of Dublin, who lobbed the ball a distance of thirty-five yards under the crossbar while Coyne rushed back to his goal line. The strong wind probably assisted the score. Galway protested that the goal should be disallowed because of the presence of Heffernan in the square. The referee allowed the goal to stand, even though he did take Heffernan's name. Rock later admitted that he thought Heffernan's presence did contribute to the score. It was a sensational, uncanny goal, styled on Mikey Sheehy's wizardry in the 1975 final and his remarkable goal scored against Paddy Cullen in the 1978 final.

Later in the game Brian Mullins was tackled by Brian Talty of Galway, and he swung his arm back at Talty, who fell to the ground. Mullins was sent off. Talty later said he could hardly remember the incident because the blow was so hard. He was concussed, but he played on until half-time. Ironically, some years later Talty became part of the Dublin back-room team, along with Brian Mullins.

Shortly before half-time a number of players became

involved in a clash, and referee John Gough decided to send off Ray Hazley of Dublin and Tomás Tierney of Galway.

Dublin led by 1–05 to 0–02 at half-time. While the players were in the tunnel, Brian Talty received a black eye. Talty has always refused to name the player who was responsible. The Galway medical team decided that he was not fit to play in the second half.

During half-time Heffernan told the Dublin players to retreat into defence when Galway had the ball, that they had to hold the ball and not make any risky passes to avoid the ball being turned over. The only Dublin player who was instructed to remain in the forward line was Joe McNally. When Dublin had the ball, Heffernan wanted them to get it to McNally as quickly as possible and to move up the field to support him. He also emphasised that Galway had only one extra man.

Five minutes after half-time Kieran Duff of Dublin lifted his foot towards the face of Pat O'Neill, who was on the ground at the time. Duff did not actually touch O'Neill but the referee decided to send him off. This left Dublin with twelve men playing Galway with fourteen. However the 'twelve apostles' or the 'defiant dozen' managed to survive and win on a score of 1–10 to 1–08. A particularly impressive score in the second half was a kick by Tommy Drumm from the Dublin back line that went over the heads of the

Galway back line into the hands of Joe McNally, who scored a point. Match reports suggest that Galway panicked. But Kevin Heffernan's tactic of packing midfield and a superb performance by Dublin's Pat Canavan both helped Dublin to win.

The GAA took some weeks to decide on how to react to the game. Kieran Duff was given a twelve-month ban and Brian Mullins received five months, Ray Hazley one month and manager Kevin Heffernan three months. Tomás Tierney and Peter Lee were both suspended for a month each. Both county boards were fined. Dublin felt that the punishments suggested that they bore more of the responsibility for the incidents, a verdict with which they did not agree.

Almost Fifty Players Warm Up in Front of Hill 16: 1984 Semi-Final

It is normal practice for the Dublin team to warm up in front of their supporters on Hill 16. But in the 1984 All-Ireland semi-final (Dublin v Tyrone), Tyrone were first on the pitch and chose to occupy that area of the pitch. When Dublin manager Kevin Heffernan received the news that Tyrone were warming up in front of the Hill, he instructed his team to 'go down to the Hill and show them that's ours!'[41] They did as they were told. Goalkeeper John O'Leary joined the Tyrone goalkeeper on the goal line. The result was that there were almost fifty players in that part of the pitch shooting at both goalkeepers.

The tactic seemed to unsettle Tyrone more than Dublin, because it was twenty-eight minutes before their first score. A goal from Barney Rock meant Dublin were ahead at half-time 1–06 to 0–02, and they went on to win on a scoreline of 2–11 to 0–08. Following the game, Tyrone described Dublin's behaviour as 'childish'.

Open-Top Bus Parade through Empty Streets Precedes Dublin Loss: 1992 Final

Amazingly, following Dublin's defeat of Clare in the 1992 semi-final, it was decided that the Dublin team should have an open-top bus parade in the city! Paul Curran described the scene:

> I remember absolutely nobody turning up; we could have been on the 77A to Tallaght. It was surreal to be honest, there wasn't a sinner. I don't know who was involved or who said 'yeah', but it was a crazy decision really ... But the reception at the Mansion House was fine; there were the usual die-hard Dublin supporters there to greet us.[42]

Tommy Carr actually refused to go on the bus at all and according to Dessie Farrell, 'The whole thing was a disaster.

We went down O'Connell Street and, sure, there were people coming back from work and they were looking about as if to say: "What are these crowd at?"' To add to the problems, in his speech at the Mansion House manager Paddy Cullen said the match was not a matter of life and death. Some players left in protest at what they regarded as cavalier words.[43]

In the final Dublin faced Donegal, whom they had beaten earlier in the year in a League quarter-final. Donegal's semi-final win against Mayo had been a very poor game. Tommy Carr remembered three Dublin players left the match early saying 'we would beat the pick of both teams'.

Dublin were in their first final since 1985 and were the favourites to win. As Carr recalled:

> We went into that without thinking we could lose and all we could see was the steps of the Hogan Stand and the Sam Maguire cup and the celebrations. That's not a criticism of a manager or the players – it's an atmosphere that descends on a team no matter how much you talk about 'we can't feel like this'. Sometimes when you talk about not taking something for granted the more you start to take it for granted.[44]

In the early minutes of the game, it seemed that Dublin would have an easy win. However, in the ninth minute, Charlie Redmond missed a penalty and Donegal recovered, going on to win the match by four points: Donegal 0–18, Dublin 0–14.

Trouble on Hill 16: 1993 Final

Cork made a great start to the 1993 final against Derry and led by 1–02 before 'Man-of-the-Match' Johnny McGurk of Derry scored his team's first point. Tony Davis of Cork was subsequently sent off in the first half and Derry went on to win by 1–14 to 2–08.

However, the most significant event of the day occurred off the pitch. Eight minutes into the match supporters were forced up against the fencing – 'trapped' was the term used in the newspaper report. The report continues:

> A gate was opened at the Canal End when it became clear a major crowd control problem had occurred. With those at the front unable to get up on to the terrace because of the crowd already there, and with others pressing forward, it appeared at one stage a serious incident was likely. St John Ambulance personnel who rushed to the scene when they saw the situation deteriorate treated several people for shock.[45]

Double Sending-Off: 1995 Final

Jason Sherlock made his debut playing for Dublin in 1995, when he was nineteen. Dublin had won their last final in

1983, when he was just seven years old. Sherlock's exotic good looks (his father was from Hong Kong), combined with his football talent, made him a media sensation, and he became the focus of adulation from younger Dublin fans.

His first big moment in the championship came in the semi-final against Cork. It arose from a controversial quick free taken by Keith Barr. Sherlock evaded Mark O'Connor's attempt to prevent him from scoring, and achieved a wonderful goal, one of the most memorable in Croke Park in the modern era.

Although Sherlock also scored in the final, the major talking point about the 1995 All-Ireland (Dublin v Tyrone) was the double sending-off of Dublin's Charlie Redmond. He was sent off but did not leave the pitch, and a minute later the referee had to send him off a second time. This breach of discipline could have formed the basis of an appeal by Tyrone against the result. The regulations stated that if such an incident occurred, the punishment would be 'forfeiture of the game and award to the opposing team'. However, Tyrone probably did not want to win their first All-Ireland by objecting.

The Dublin manager, Pat O'Neill, initially thought the game was a draw. He did not realise that a point scored by Tyrone's Seán McLaughlin had been disallowed. McLaughlin scored a point from a pass by Peter Canavan, but the referee decided that Canavan had touched the ball on the ground, and Dublin had beaten Tyrone by a point: 1–10 to 0–12.[46]

Replayed Final: 1996

The 1996 final between Meath and Mayo on 15 September 1996 resulted in a draw, with a score of Meath 0–12, Mayo 1–09. Previous to the match Mayo had objected to the appointment of Pat McEnaney as referee because of his business contacts with Meath, but he was still given the job and officiated in both matches. It was an appointment he may later have regretted.

The replay of the final two weeks later became notorious for a brawl that broke out in front of the Meath goal, involving many of the players from both teams. The fight started after a series of fouls committed on Meath's nineteen-year-old player Darren Fay. Almost thirty players joined in the brawl, which will go down as one of the worst ever seen at a GAA match. When the situation was finally brought under control, Pat McEnaney sought to punish those he deemed the worst offenders: 'When it all settled down my gut instinct was to send off [Meath's John] McDermott with [Mayo's Liam] McHale. I had my mind made up on that,' McEnaney later said. Then he consulted with umpire Francie McMahon, who had witnessed something dreadful. 'Pat,' he said. 'You're going to have to send off [Meath's] Colm Coyle. He's after dropping about six of them.' One of the linesmen, Kevin Walsh, also intervened to highlight Coyle's alleged indiscretions.[47] In the end it was McHale and Coyle who were shown red cards.

Meath had been behind from the tenth minute of the game, but they went ahead with a penalty by Trevor Giles in the sixty-fourth minute and a point from Tommy Dowd. Mayo equalised very late in the game, but Giles won the ball, which allowed Brendan Reilly to score the winning point for Meath. The final result was Meath 2–09, Mayo 1–11.

Maurice Magnificent against Mayo: 1997 Final

In the 1997 final (Kerry v Mayo), Kerry were dominant and in front until Mayo's Ciarán McDonald scored a penalty and Mayo also scored two points to bring the gap back to one point in the fifty-first minute. However, Mayo failed to score again in the time remaining.

As Páidí Ó Sé wrote, Kerry was a little uncertain following Mayo's scores, and 'then there was Maurice, and Maurice again. This was his stage. He was absolutely magnificent.'[48] The match could be described as Maurice Fitzgerald's final, as he scored nine points in total. Kerry won the game 0–13 to 1–7, which meant that Fitzgerald's points were crucial. His performance won him the 'Man-of-the-Match' award, and he was also chosen as 'Footballer of the Year' in that year's All-Star awards.

New Structure for the Championship: 2001

In 2001 the structure of the championship was changed in a way that separated the All-Ireland Championship from the provincial championships. Rather than the knock-out system that was in place previously, all the losers at the provincial stage would now compete in a new round of qualifiers for the right to play the provincial winners at the All-Ireland quarter-final stage.

In the year it was introduced, Galway became the first team to win the championship using the new system. They were beaten by Roscommon in the Connacht semi-final, but in the qualifiers they beat Wicklow, Armagh and Cork to claim their place in the All-Ireland quarter-finals. There they faced Roscommon again, but this time emerged as winners.

Their opponents in the final were Meath. The first half of the game was of poor quality – the teams both scored six points and had a large number of wides. However, in the second half Galway in particular improved the standard of their play and were leading by five points late in the second half when Meath were awarded a crucial penalty. Luckily for Galway, Trevor Giles missed the goal and the Connacht team went on to win convincingly. Pádraic Joyce was the star of the game, scoring ten points in total. The final score was Galway 0–17, Meath 0–08.

Introduction of the Qualifiers in the All-Ireland Championship, 2001

The second-chance qualification introduced in 2001 has produced quite a few All-Ireland winners:

2001: Galway 0–17 to 0–08 Meath – Galway came from round two, beating Wicklow, Armagh and Cork.

2005: Tyrone 1–16 to 2–10 Kerry – Tyrone came from round four to defeat holders Kerry.

2006: Kerry 4–15 to 3–05 Mayo – Kerry came from round four of the qualifiers to take the title.

2008: Tyrone 1–15 to 0–14 Kerry – Tyrone came from round two and beat Kerry, who came via round three.

2009: Kerry 0–16 to 1–09 Cork – Second All-Munster final; Kerry came from round two to defeat Cork.

2010: Cork 0–16 to 0–15 Down – Every provincial winner lost in the quarter-finals; the finalists came from round two.

Armagh Manager's Striking Half-Time Speech: 2002 Final

In the 2002 final Armagh trailed Kerry by 0–11 to 0–07 at half-time, but Armagh manager Joe Kernan was prepared for this situation. He had played on the Armagh team that lost the 1977 final (Dublin 5–12, Armagh 3–06) and had been given a loser's plaque. Before the 2002 match he had obtained a winner's medal, and during a rousing half-time speech he threw his plaque against the wall and produced the winner's medal, insisting that Armagh could win the second half to get a winner's medal.

Kerry were left alone on the field for minutes after the half-time break ended while Kernan was making his speech, which clearly worked as intended. Oisin McConville had missed a penalty in the first half, but compensated by scoring a goal in the fifty-fifth minute to reduce the gap to one point. Armagh then went on to secure victory with two points scored by Ronan Clarke and Steven McDonnell. It was the first time that Armagh had won an All-Ireland final, having lost the finals in 1953 and 1977. The final score was Armagh 1–12, Kerry 0–14.

First Final Featuring Two Teams from the Same Province: 2003

The 2003 final was the first year in which two teams from the same province – in this case, Ulster – played each other. This scenario had only been made possible because of the new 'back-door' system brought in in 2001. Armagh were the reigning champions, while Tyrone had yet to win a final, having lost in 1986 against Kerry and in 1995 against Dublin.

Before the break Tyrone led by 0–08 to 0–04. Five of Tyrone's points had been scored by Peter Canavan from frees. However, he had to be taken off at half-time due to the recurrence of an ankle injury he had suffered in the semi-final against Kerry.

In the second half Diarmuid Marsden of Armagh was sent off after an off-the-ball incident. On appeal to the central council, the suspension was overturned after the fact. Both teams played in a very defensive manner and there were numerous stoppages for injuries, plus accusations of diving (if the referee is fooled and gives a free kick, the 'diver' has achieved his objective). For Tyrone, Peter Canavan came back on to replace Gerard Cavlan for the last ten minutes of the match. Tyrone managed to hang on to their lead, and although Armagh reduced that lead to two points at one stage, Tyrone eventually won 0–12 to 0–09. While most commentators considered it a poor-quality game, this would hardly have dampened Tyrone's joy at winning their first All-Ireland Football Championship. Peter Canavan became the first player from Tyrone to accept the Sam Maguire Cup.

Kerry Back on the Summit: 2004 Final

The 2004 All-Ireland final (Kerry v Mayo) is remembered as a very disappointing game. Despite the fact that Mayo's Alan

Dillon scored a goal after five minutes, Kerry led by 1–12 to 1–04 at half-time. Their scores included a great goal by Colm (Gooch) Cooper after twenty-five minutes following a pass from Éamon Fitzmaurice. Some spectators even left at half-time, so certain were they that Kerry would win, and the stadium was reported to be one-third empty at full time. Kerry won by 1–20 to Mayo's 2–09.

Martin Breheny wrote in the *Irish Independent*:

> So then, after three miserable years in which Croke Park was a scene of desolation for Kerry, they are back on the summit, having won the National League, Munster and All-Ireland treble for the first time since 1997.
>
> They completed the haul with a style and fluency that suggested they had plenty more in reserve if Mayo managed to raise their game. But it wasn't necessary since Mayo froze solid after getting off to the best possible start.[49]

Clash with Ryder Cup Delays Final: 2005

In contrast to the previous year's final, 2005's match between Tyrone and Kerry is considered to be one of the best. The game was postponed by a week from the traditional date for the All-Ireland final (the third weekend of September), as golf's Ryder Cup was to be played at The K Club in Kildare that weekend, and 35,000 people were expected to attend the golf, placing extra demand on hotel accommodation in Dublin and putting severe pressure on public transport.

Kerry were attempting to complete another three-in-a-row. They had a great start: Dara Ó Cinnéide scored a goal after six minutes and Colm Cooper had some fine scores in the early part of the match. But Tyrone reversed the trend in the second quarter, when they scored 1–05 to Kerry's 0–02. The goal was scored by Peter Canavan, who was taken off at the break but once again reappeared in the fifty-fifth minute and scored a point at a crucial time in the game. Tyrone ensured a great win, scoring 1–16 to Kerry's 2–10.

First Final between Teams Beaten in the Championship: 2008

The 2008 final, once again between Tyrone and Kerry, was the first between two teams beaten in the provincial championships. Between them, these two teams had already dominated the All-Irelands in the first decade of this century, with Kerry winning in 2000, 2004, 2006 and 2007, and Tyrone in 2003 and 2005.

Having made it through the qualifiers, Tyrone had defeated Wexford in the All-Ireland semi-final and Kerry had overcome Cork in a replay of their semi-final. Kerry were yet again looking for another three-in-a-row, but Tyrone were destined to dash their run for glory. Although Kerry were leading by a point at half-time, they had already had six wides to Tyrone's one. Kerry continued to use the strategy of the high ball in – that is, kicking the ball high in the air over a long distance, over the heads of most players, with the intention that it will be captured by a member of the same team, in Kerry's case Kieran Donaghy or Tommy Walsh. Match reports later suggested that it was this use of the high-ball-in strategy that contributed to their defeat. Despite this, there was just one point in it with four minutes to go, but a great save by Tyrone goalkeeper Pascal McConnell from a shot at goal by Declan O'Sullivan helped to give Tyrone the win: 1–15 to 0–14.

125th Anniversary of the GAA's foundation: 2009 Final

In 2009 – the 125th-anniversary year of the foundation of the GAA – Cork and Kerry contested the All-Ireland final. Cork began very well, leading 1–03 to 0–01 after eleven minutes. However, in the words of Martin Breheny in the *Irish Independent:*

> … it was no more than a mirage which faded quickly once Kerry secured the defensive bolts and set about applying consistent pressure to a Cork defence which had looked so sturdy all summer. The difference this time was that Cork's

vaunted half-back line of Noel O'Leary, Graham Canty and John Miskella who had dominated previous opposition with their stampeding runs, now found themselves having to think a whole lot more about their defensive duties.

With that trio facing their own problems, Cork were unable to generate the same levels of momentum which took them to the final.[50]

Cork should have performed better, but as their confidence levels sagged in the second half, their shooting disintegrated into what Breheny called an 'embarrassing mess'. The final score was Kerry 0–16, Cork 1–09. Kerry was victorious once again on a significant anniversary for the GAA – they had also won in the 75th- and 100th-anniversary years.

Mícheál Ó Muircheartaigh's Final Commentary: 2010 Final

The 2010 final between Cork and Down was the last final for which esteemed commentator Mícheál Ó Muircheartaigh provided the commentary. He had announced his retirement six days earlier.

Before this game, Down had won all five finals in which they had played. If they were to win, they would have the same number of victories as Cork, who had won the championship six times since it started in 1887. Cork had lost two finals to Kerry in the previous three years.

It was the first time these teams had met in the final. As both wore red jerseys, it was decided that both teams would wear their 'away' jerseys: Cork's was white with a red trim, and Down's yellow with a red-and-black trim.

In the first half Down were leading 0–07 to 0–02 after twenty-seven minutes, but Cork's Daniel Goulding and Donncha O'Connor scored two points just before half-time, so Cork were only three points behind at the break. The decision by Cork to bring on Nicholas Murphy and Graham Canty helped them to dominate the second half and Daniel Goulding scored three forty-fives (when a player or the goalkeeper puts the ball over the end line, the opposing team is given a free from the forty-five metre line, hence the term a 'forty-five'). Although Down's Benny Coulter and Daniel Hughes scored in the last minutes, Cork won by a point, 0–16 to 0–15. The *Sunday Game* panel selected Daniel Goulding as 'Man of the Match'.

Victory for Dublin Following Sixteen-Year Journey 'To Hell and Back': 2011 Final

By the 2011 final between Dublin and Kerry, Dublin had not won for sixteen years, and their captain Bryan Cullen said the team had been 'to hell and back over the last few years'.[51] At 4.53 p.m. Kerry was leading 1–10 to 0–09, and were in 'cruise control', heading for victory. Then Dublin put Kevin McManamon on the field. Receiving a pass from Alan Brogan, he forced his way through the Kerry defence to score a goal. Points from Kevin Nolan and Alan Brogan gave Dublin the lead. Kerry's Kieran Donaghy made the scores equal in the seventieth minute, which meant the game was heading to the first final draw since 2000. McManamon then won a free thirty-eight metres from the Kerry goal. Stephen Cluxton, the Dublin goalkeeper, took the free to score the winning point. The result: Dublin 1–12, Kerry 1–11. Cluxton had scored eleven points in the championship, making him Dublin's fourth-highest scorer. Kevin Nolan was named 'Man of the Match'.

'See yiz in Coppers!' roared Dublin skipper Cullen at the end of his speech.[52]

A Win for Donegal Twenty Years after their First: 2012 Final

In the 2012 semi-finals Mayo beat Dublin, the reigning champions, setting up a final with Donegal, who had beaten Cork. Two minutes and twenty-five seconds into the final, Donegal's Michael Murphy scored an incredible goal. Murphy was on the edge of the square when Karl Lacey sent a high ball towards him. The Donegal captain leapt for the ball, holding off Kevin Keane and fired the ball into the net.[53] It was later named as goal of the championship by the RTÉ programme *Championship Matters*. After ten minutes, a mistake by Kevin Keane of Mayo allowed Donegal's Colm McFadden to score a second goal. Mayo finally got on the scoreboard with a point from a short free from Alan Dillon passed to Kevin McLoughlin after sixteen minutes, but they faced an uphill battle. McFadden scored 1–03 in the first half, and by half-time the score was Donegal 2–04, Mayo 0–06. Mayo never recovered from being so far behind and the final score was Donegal 2–11, Mayo 0–13 – Donegal's second victory in the championship, twenty years after their first. Mayo's run of defeats continued. 'Man of the Match' was Michael Murphy of Donegal.

Hawk-Eye's First Appearance at a Final: 2013

The 2013 final between Dublin and Mayo was the first to use 'Hawk-Eye' technology. The GAA had introduced this technology in Croke Park in 2013 to deal with a problem: when the ball is kicked over the bar to score a point, it can be very difficult for the umpires to be sure that it has gone between the posts. Hawk-Eye uses four high-speed cameras at each end to locate the position of the ball up to twenty-six metres above the posts and four metres outside each post. Thus it removes the uncertainty about whether or not it is a score. Hawk-Eye's first decision was to rule that a kick by Keith Higgins of Mayo had gone wide.

In the first half of the match both teams wasted possession – Dublin had ten wides and Mayo nine. While Mayo appeared to dominate possession, they could not convert this dominance into scores. However, they led at half-time by a point: Mayo 0–08, Dublin 1–04. Dublin's goal was scored by Bernard Brogan.

Dublin got off to the better start in the second half, when a kick from Eoghan O'Gara was saved by Mayo's Robert Hennelly, but went over the bar. Dublin pulled ahead, but after fifteen minutes, a goal by Andy Moran of Mayo made both teams level, at 1–09 each. Then, four minutes later, Bernard Brogan scored another goal. Approaching the end of the game, Mayo were two points behind when they were awarded a close-in free (one that is within easy scoring distance for the kicker of the ball to score a point). However, Cillian O'Connor went for a point instead of a goal. The referee blew the final whistle following Stephen Cluxton's kick-out. The final score was Dublin 2–12, Mayo 1–14. Bernard Brogan of Dublin was the 'Man of the Match' and Dublin were back on top.

9

SAM MAGUIRE CUP MISCELLANY OF FACTS AND FIGURES

List of Winners

Below is a list of the number of times each county has won the Sam Maguire Cup from 1928, when it was first awarded, up to 2016 inclusive, which makes a total of eighty-nine finals. Only sixteen of the counties involved in the championship have won the cup.

Team	Number of wins	Percentage of wins
Kerry	30	33.71%
Dublin	12	13.48%
Galway	8	8.99%
Meath	7	7.87%
Down	5	5.62%
Cork	5	5.62%

Team	Number of wins	Percentage of wins
Cavan	5	5.62%
Offaly	3	3.37%
Tyrone	3	3.37%
Mayo	3	3.37%
Roscommon	2	2.25%
Donegal	2	2.25%
Louth	1	1.12%
Armagh	1	1.12%
Derry	1	1.12%
Kildare	1	1.12%

Of the thirty-two counties, just half have won the cup. If New York and London are included, the percentage of successful counties falls to 47 per cent.

The Pareto Effect or 80/20 Effect

There is a statistical phenomenon known as the Pareto effect, or 80/20 effect, which states that around 80 per cent of effects come from 20 per cent of causes. This phenomenon can be applied to the winning teams' figures:

Team	Number of wins	Percentage of wins	Cumulative percentage of wins
Kerry	30	33.71%	33.71%
Dublin	12	13.48%	47.19%

Team	Number of wins	Percentage of wins	Cumulative percentage of wins
Galway	8	8.99%	56.18%
Meath	7	7.87%	64.04%
Down	5	5.62%	69.66%
Cork	5	5.62%	75.28%
Cavan	5	5.62%	80.90%

The final column shows that seven teams have won the cup on 80.9 per cent of the occasions on which it has been contested; seven teams are twenty per cent of the thirty-four teams. So twenty per cent of teams have won eighty per cent of All-Irelands since 1928.

Greatest Football Teams

The Team of the Century was nominated in 1984 by *Sunday Independent* readers and selected by a panel of experts, including journalists and former players. It was chosen as part of the GAA's centenary year celebrations:

Goalkeeper
Dan O'Keeffe
(Kerry)

Right Corner-Back
Enda Colleran
(Galway)

Full-Back
Paddy O'Brien
(Meath)

Left Corner-Back
Seán Flanagan
(Mayo)

Right Half-Back
Seán Murphy
(Kerry)

Centre-Back
John Joe O'Reilly
(Cavan)

Left Half-Back
Stephen White
(Louth)

Midfield
Mick O'Connell
(Kerry)

Jack O'Shea
(Kerry)

Right Half-Forward
Seán O'Neill
(Down)

Centre-Forward
Seán Purcell
(Galway)

Left Half-Forward
Pat Spillane
(Kerry)

Right Corner-Forward
Mikey Sheehy
(Kerry)

Full-Forward
Tommy Langan
(Mayo)

Left Corner-Forward
Kevin Heffernan
(Dublin)

The Team of the Millennium was a team chosen in 1999 by a panel of GAA past presidents and journalists. The goal was to single out the best-ever fifteen players who had played the game in their respective positions:

Goalkeeper
Dan O'Keeffe
(Kerry)

Right Corner-Back
Enda Colleran
(Galway)

Full-Back
Joe Keohane
(Kerry)

Left Corner-Back
Seán Flanagan
(Mayo)

Right Half-Back
Seán Murphy
(Kerry)

Centre-Back
John Joe O'Reilly
(Cavan)

Left Half-Back
Martin O'Connell
(Meath)

Midfield
Mick O'Connell
(Kerry)

Tommy Murphy
(Laois)

Right Half-Forward
Seán O'Neill
(Down)

Centre-Forward
Seán Purcell
(Galway)

Left Half-Forward
Pat Spillane
(Kerry)

Right Corner-Forward
Mikey Sheehy
(Kerry)

Full-Forward
Tommy Langan
(Mayo)

Left Corner-Forward
Kevin Heffernan
(Dublin)

Players Selected on Both Teams:

Twelve players were selected for both the Team of the Century and the Team of the Millennium. Here is a list of the finals they won:

Dan O'Keeffe (Kerry): 1931, 1932, 1937, 1939, 1940, 1941, 1946

Enda Colleran (Galway): 1964, 1965, 1966

Seán Flanagan (Mayo): 1950, 1951

Seán Murphy (Kerry): 1953, 1955, 1959

J. J. O'Reilly (Cavan): 1947, 1948

Mick O'Connell (Kerry): 1959, 1962, 1969, 1970

Seán O'Neill (Down): 1960, 1961,1968

Seán Purcell (Galway): 1956

Pat Spillane (Kerry): 1975, 1978, 1979, 1980, 1981, 1984, 1985, 1986

Mikey Sheehy (Kerry): 1975, 1978, 1979, 1980, 1981, 1984, 1985, 1986

Tommy Langan (Mayo): 1950, 1951

Kevin Heffernan (Dublin): 1958

Players Who Have Won Eight Winners Medals in the All-Ireland Final since 1928

Five players, all from Kerry, have won eight medals in the All-Ireland finals for which the Sam Maguire Cup was awarded:

Denis (Ogie) Moran (Kerry and Beale) – the only player to win his medals in the same position, centre half-forward: 1975, 1978, 1979, 1980, 1981, 1984, 1985, 1986

Ger Power (Kerry and Austin Stacks): 1975, 1978, 1979, 1980, 1981, 1984, 1985, 1986

Mikey Sheehy (Kerry and Austin Stacks): 1975, 1978, 1979, 1980, 1981, 1984, 1985, 1986

Páidí Ó Sé (Kerry and An Ghaeltacht): 1975, 1978, 1979, 1980, 1981, 1984, 1985, 1986

Pat Spillane (Kerry and Templenoe): 1975, 1978, 1979, 1980, 1981, 1984, 1985, 1986

Players Who Have Been Presented with the Cup on More than One Occasion

Only eight men have had the honour of being presented with the trophy twice as captain, and only one man, Stephen Cluxton of Dublin, has had that honour on three occasions:

Player	County	Club	Years
Joe Barrett	Kerry	Austin Stacks	1929, 1932
Jimmy Murray	Roscommon	St Patrick's	1943, 1944
John Joe O'Reilly	Cavan	Cornafean	1947, 1948
Seán Flanagan	Mayo	Ballaghaderreen	1950, 1951
Enda Colleran	Galway	Mountbellew/ Moylough	1965, 1966
Tony Hanahoe	Dublin	St Vincent's	1976, 1977
Brian Dooher	Tyrone	Clann na nGael	2005, 2008
Declan O'Sullivan	Kerry	Dromid Pearses	2006, 2007
Stephen Cluxton	Dublin	Parnells	2013, 2015, 2016

Texaco Footballer of the Year

The Texaco Footballer of the Year award was made to the player considered to be the best footballer of that year's All-Ireland Championship. The player was selected by a group of journalists on television and the print media. The award was first given in 1958 and was discontinued in 2012 when Texaco withdrew the sponsorship.

The first recipient was Jim McKeever of Derry, who captained Derry in the 1958 final against Dublin. His usual position was midfield, and he was described by Mick O'Connell as the greatest catcher of a ball he ever marked.

Three players won the award despite the fact that their county did not win that year's All-Ireland: Jim McKeever (Derry, 1958), Colm O'Rourke (Meath, 1991) and Bernard Brogan (Dublin, 2010). Brogan's brother Alan won it in 2011.

Only one manager, Kevin Heffernan (Dublin), won the award, in 1974.

Two men won it twice: James McCartan (Down, 1960 and 1961) and Jimmy Keaveney (Dublin, 1976 and 1977).

Jack O'Shea (Kerry) won it the most, being awarded the accolade on four occasions: 1980, 1981, 1984 and 1985.

GPA Footballer of the Year

The Gaelic Players Association (GPA), founded in 1999, is the representative body for players who are members of county teams. The GPA Footballer of the Year award began in 2001, an award based on a vote by GPA members and thus considered one of the greatest honours that can be won by a player. The recipients of this award so far are:

2001: Pádraic Joyce (Galway)
2002: Kieran McGeeney (Armagh)

2003: Steven McDonnell (Armagh; did not win the All-Ireland that year)

2004: Mattie Forde (Wexford; did not win the All-Ireland that year)

2005: Stephen O'Neill (Tyrone)

2006: Kieran Donaghy (Kerry)

2007: Marc Ó Sé (Kerry)

2008: Seán Cavanagh (Tyrone)

2009: Paul Galvin (Kerry)

2010: Bernard Brogan (Dublin; did not win the All-Ireland that year)

2011: Alan Brogan (Dublin)

2012: Karl Lacey (Donegal)

2013: Michael Darragh MacAuley (Dublin; the first time it was presented in Croke Park)

2014: James O'Donoghue (Kerry)

2015: Jack McCaffrey (Dublin; young player of the year 2013)

2016: Lee Keegan (Mayo; did not win the All-Ireland that year)

GAA/GPA Football All-Stars

At the end of each season the best players are selected for the GAA/GPA All-Stars team. Forty-five players from different counties are chosen as the best in a specific position by a panel of sports journalists from the Irish media. The fifteen members of the team are then voted for by the members of the GPA. The winners are awarded an individual trophy, and the team receive a trip to the USA or Australia to play exhibition games. The All-Stars team is usually dominated by members of the two teams that make it to the All-Ireland final, but any player from any team can be included if they are judged to have played exceptionally well. In 2016 the All-Stars were dominated by the winners Dublin and runners-up Mayo, but the team also included players from Tyrone, Tipperary, Kerry and Donegal:

1   David Clarke (Mayo)
2   Brendan Harrison (Mayo)
3   Jonny Cooper (Dublin)
4   Philly McMahon (Dublin)
5   Lee Keegan (Mayo)
6   Colm Boyle (Mayo)
7   Ryan McHugh (Donegal)
8   Brian Fenton (Dublin)
9   Mattie Donnelly (Tyrone)
10 Peter Harte (Tyrone)
11 Diarmuid Connolly (Dublin)
12 Ciaran Kilkenny (Dublin)
13 Dean Rock (Dublin)
14 Michael Quinlivan (Tipperary)
15 Paul Geaney (Kerry)

There are also All-Stars awards for ladies football, hurling, camogie and rounders.

Fastest Goals in the Final

The goal scored by Garry McMahon (Kerry) after thirty-four seconds of the 1962 All-Ireland final is the fastest in the history of the All-Ireland Senior Football Championship final. Other quick goals include:

1973: Jimmy Barry-Murphy (Cork): 2 minutes

1975: John Egan (Kerry): 3 minutes

1980: John O'Connor (Roscommon): 35 seconds

1993: Joe Kavanagh (Cork): 5 minutes

2004: Alan Dillon (Mayo): 4 minutes

2005: Dara Ó Cinnéide (Kerry): 6 minutes

2012: Michael Murphy (Donegal): 3 minutes

2014: Paul Geaney (Kerry): 49 seconds

Largest Winning Margins

The largest winning margin was eighteen points, in 1930 and again in 1936. Below are the details of these games and other finals with high winning margins.

Year	Winning Team	Losing Team	Winning Margin
1930	Kerry (3–11)	Monaghan (0–02)	18 points
1936	Mayo (4–11)	Laois (0–05)	18 points
1977	Dublin (5–12)	Armagh (3–06)	12 points
1978	Kerry (5–11)	Dublin (0–09)	17 points
1979	Kerry (3–13)	Dublin (1–08)	11 points

Most Successful Provincial Teams

The most successful provincial teams are as follows:

Province	Teams with Most All-Ireland Senior Football Championship Titles since 1928
Ulster	Cavan and Down
Leinster	Dublin
Connacht	Galway
Munster	Kerry

Finals Featuring Two Teams from the Same Province

Only on three occasions has the All-Ireland Senior Football Championship final been contested by two teams from the same province:

Ulster: Tyrone v Armagh (2003)

Munster: Kerry v Cork (2007)

Munster: Kerry v Cork (2009)

Record Attendance

The largest attendance was for the 1961 final between Down and Offaly: 90,556 spectators.

Consecutive Wins

The ten counties that have won the cup on consecutive occasions are:

Kerry (four in a row – twice; treble – twice; double – twice)

Galway (treble)

Dublin (double – twice)

Roscommon (double)

Cavan (double)

Mayo (double)

Down (double)

Offaly (double)

Cork (double)

Meath (double)

The first four-in-a-row was achieved by Kerry by winning the final in the years 1929 to 1932:

1929: Kerry 1–08, Kildare 1–05

1930: Kerry 3–11, Monaghan 0–02

1931: Kerry 1–11, Kildare 0–08

1932: Kerry 2–07, Mayo 2–04

Cavan surprisingly beat Kerry in the All-Ireland semi-final in 1933, when they went on to win their first final.

Kerry's second four-in-a-row was from 1978 to 1981:

1978: Kerry 5–11, Dublin 0–09

1979: Kerry 3–13, Dublin 1–08

1980: Kerry 1–09, Roscommon 1–06
1981: Kerry 1–12, Offaly 0–08

Kerry achieved three-in-a-row from 1939 to 1941:

1939: Kerry 2–05, Meath 2–03
1940: Kerry 0–07, Galway 1–03
1941: Kerry 1–08, Galway 0–07

Kerry's second treble ran from 1984 to 1986:

1984: Kerry 0–14, Dublin 1–06
1985: Kerry 2–12, Dublin 2–08
1986: Kerry 2–15, Tyrone 1–10

Galway's treble came in 1964, 1965 and 1966:

1964: Galway 0–15, Kerry 0–10
1965: Galway 0–12, Kerry 0–09
1966: Galway 1–10, Meath 0–07

Roscommon's double:

1943: Roscommon 2–07, Cavan 2–02
1944: Roscommon 1–09, Kerry 2–04

Cavan's double:
1947: Cavan 2–11, Kerry 2–07
1948: Cavan 4–05, Mayo 4–04

Mayo's double:

1950: Mayo 2–05, Louth 1–06
1951: Mayo 2–08, Meath 0–09

Down's double:

1960: Down 2–10, Kerry 0–08
1961: Down 3–06, Offaly 2–08

Kerry's first double:

1969: Kerry 0–10, Offaly 0–07
1970: Kerry 2–19, Meath 0–18

Offaly's double:

1971: Offaly 1–14, Galway 2–08
1972: Offaly 1–19, Kerry 0–13

Dublin's first double:

1976: Dublin 3–08, Kerry 0–10
1977: Dublin 5–12, Armagh 3–06

Meath's double:

1987: Meath 1–14, Cork 0–11
1988: Meath 0–13, Cork 0–12

Cork's double:

1989: Cork 0–17, Mayo 1–11
1990: Cork 0–11, Meath 0–09

The year 1990 saw the first and only 'double' of the Sam Maguire Cup era, when Cork won both the hurling and football championships. Teddy McCarthy is the only player to have won medals in both finals in one year.

Kerry's second double:

2006: Kerry 4–15, Mayo 3–05
2007: Kerry 3–13, Cork 1–09

Dublin's second double:

2015: Dublin 0–12, Kerry 0–09
2016: Dublin 1–15, Mayo 1–14

Sam Maguire Cup Won after a Replay

As Gaelic football has no provision to deal with a draw at the end of a match, the game has to be replayed. This has happened on ten occasions since the cup has been presented.

Year	Replay Winner	Loser	Winning Margin
1937	Kerry	Cavan	6 points
1938	Galway	Kerry	3 points

Year	Replay Winner	Loser	Winning Margin
1943	Roscommon	Cavan	5 points
1946	Kerry	Roscommon	4 points
1952	Cavan	Meath	4 points
1972	Offaly	Kerry	9 points
1988	Meath	Cork	1 point
1996	Meath	Mayo	1 point
2000	Kerry	Galway	4 points
2016	Dublin	Mayo	1 point

Players Who Have Lost in Four or More All-Ireland Finals without Winning One

Alan Dillon (Mayo): 2004, 2006, 2012, 2013, 2016. In his first final Dillon scored a goal after four minutes.

James Nallen (Mayo): 1996, 1997, 2004, 2006. He was taken off in the final in 2006 and actually played in five All-Ireland finals, if you count the All-Ireland final replay against Meath in 1996.

Andy Moran (Mayo): 2004, 2006, 2012, 2013, 2016.

Keith Higgins (Mayo): 2006, 2012, 2013, 2016.

Tommy Joe Gilmore (Galway): 1971, 1973, 1974, 1983 (one as sub).

Billy Joyce (Galway): 1971, 1973, 1974, 1983 (one as sub).[1]

Players Who Have Lost in Three All-Ireland Finals without Winning One

David Brady (Mayo): 1996, 2004, 2006. He did not play during the 1997 season.

Ciarán McDonald (Mayo): 1997, 2004, 2006. He began his Mayo career in 1994 and was dropped in 2007. This period encompassed four Mayo All-Ireland final appearances, but McDonald was out of action for the 1996 season.

Dermot Flanagan and Liam McHale (Mayo): 1989, 1996, 1997. The year 1989 saw Mayo's first final appearance in decades.

Gay Mitchell, Joe Waldron, Liam O'Neill, Tom Naughton, Brendan Colleran (Galway): 1971, 1973, 1974.

Johnny Hughes (Galway): 1973, 1974, and 1983. Hughes started the 1983 All-Ireland final against Dublin even though he was not fit.[2]

Best Players of the Twenty-First Century Never to Win an All-Ireland

Brendan McVeigh, goalkeeper, Down

Seán Marty Lockhart, right corner-back, Derry

Barry Owens, full-back, Fermanagh

Joe Higgins, left corner-back, Laois

Aaron Kernan, right half-back, Armagh

Glen Ryan, centre half-back, Kildare

Kevin Cassidy, left half-back, Donegal

Ciárán Whelan, midfield, Dublin

Dermot Earley, midfield, Kildare

Johnny Doyle, right half-forward, Kildare

Éamonn O'Hara, centre-forward, Sligo

Dessie Dolan, left half-forward, Westmeath

Declan Browne, right corner-forward, Tipperary

Matty Forde, full-forward, Wexford

Benny Coulter, left corner-forward, Down[3]

Sent Off

The player with the distinction of being the first player to be sent off during an All-Ireland football final was Joe Stafford of Cavan in the 1943 final between Roscommon and Cavan (Roscommon 2–07, Cavan 2–02).

John Donnellan of Galway was sent off during the 1965 All-Ireland between Galway and Kerry. A unique occurrence in this match was that two brothers, Derry and John (Thorny) O'Shea of Kerry, were also both sent off (Galway 0–12, Kerry 0–09).

In 1978 the Kerry goalkeeper, Charlie Nelligan, was sent off and 'replaced' by Pat Spillane. John McCarthy of Dublin was also sent off (Kerry 5–11, Dublin 0–9).

In the 1983 final, four players were sent off: Brian Mullins, Ray Hazley and Kieran Duff of Dublin, and Tomás Tierney of Galway. The remaining twelve Dublin players, christened the 'twelve apostles', still managed to beat the remaining fourteen men of Galway (Dublin 1–10, Galway 1–08).

The strangest case is that of Charlie Redmond of Dublin, who was sent off in the 1995 final between Dublin and Tyrone, but controversially remained on the pitch for a minute after he had been dismissed. The referee later said he would also have sent off Fergal Lohan, the Tyrone player involved in the incident, except that he had not seen his jersey number. He asked the linesman if he had seen the number, but he replied, 'No.' Redmond chose to interpret this as a reply to the question 'Did Redmond commit a foul?' and stayed on the pitch. The referee restarted the match, subsequently claiming he did not see Redmond.[4] A few seconds later, when Redmond sent the ball downfield, the referee noticed his presence and asked the linesman if he had gone off. When the answer was 'No', he sent him off for second time. (Dublin 1–10, Tyrone 0–12).

Other players sent off include:

Páidí Ó Sé (Kerry), 1979 final (Kerry 3–13, Dublin 1–08)

Gerry McEntee (Meath), 1988 final replay (Meath 0–13, Cork 0–12)

Tony Davis (Cork), 1993 final (Derry 1–14, Cork 2–08)

Liam McHale (Mayo) and Colm Coyle (Meath), 1996 final replay (Meath 2–09, Mayo 1–11)

Nigel Nestor (Meath), 2001 final (Galway 0–17, Meath 0–08)

Diarmuid Marsden (Armagh), 2003 final (Tyrone 0–12, Armagh 0–09)

Black Cards

The GAA rules and regulations explain black cards as follows:

> A black card is issued by the referee to a player for any offence
> which involves tripping a player or dragging him down with
> his arms or legs, as well as for any deliberate collision in an
> attempt to take a player out of the game or disrupt the flow
> of the move.
>
> The black card will mean that a player has to leave the pitch
> and be replaced by a substitute, but if a team receives three
> black cards they won't be able to replace the next player who
> commits an offence worthy of a black card. If one player racks
> up three black cards across the season, they'll also receive a
> one-match suspension.[5]

Five players have received black cards during All-Ireland
finals: Johnny Buckley and Aidan O'Mahony (Kerry) in the
2014 and 2015 finals respectively; and Jonny Cooper (Dublin) and Rob Hennelly and Lee Keegan (Mayo) in the 2016
replay.

Penalties

The penalty kick was first suggested for soccer by an Irishman,
William McCrum, who played as a goalkeeper for Milford
Everton FC of the Irish Football League from 1890 to 1891.

Soccer began in the public schools in England and it was assumed that a gentleman would not commit a deliberate foul. True to its gentlemanly beginnings, in soccer the two team captains originally settled disputes, but, as the stakes grew, so did the number of complaints. The referee, at first, stood on the touchline keeping time and was 'referred' to if the umpires could not agree. However, that all changed in 1891. From that date, a single person with the power to send players off, as well as give penalties and free kicks without listening to appeals, became a permanent fixture in the game. The two umpires became linesmen, or 'assistant referees' as they are called today.

The penalty kick was introduced into Gaelic football in 1940. Notable penalties include:

1948: The first penalty awarded in an All-Ireland final. Pádraig Carney of Mayo scored it against Cavan (Cavan 4–05, Mayo 4–04).

1953: Armagh's Bill McCorry missed a penalty in a very tight match (Kerry 0–13, Armagh 1–06).

1960: Down's Paddy Doherty won a free by being fouled in the square. He took the penalty and beat Kerry goalkeeper Johnny Culloty (Down 2–10, Kerry 0–08).

1974: Dublin goalkeeper Paddy Cullen saved Galway's Liam Sammon's penalty kick (Dublin 0–14, Galway 1–06).

1982: Mikey Sheehy's penalty for Kerry was crucially saved by Offaly's Martin Furlong in the second half of the All-Ireland final (Offaly 1–15, Kerry 0–17).

1985: Jack O'Shea scored to help Kerry beat Dublin (Kerry 2–12, Dublin 2–08).

1992: Dublin were awarded a penalty after seven minutes of the All-Ireland final against Donegal. Charlie Redmond chipped his shot over the bar. Dublin later lost the initiative and the game (Donegal 0–18, Dublin 0–14).

1994: Dublin's Charlie Redmond hit the ball straight at the Down goalkeeper and hit the rebound wide as he was obstructed by his teammate Johnny Barr. Down went on to win the game. Redmond went straight home after the match without changing or having a shower (Down 1–12, Dublin 0–13).[6]

1996: In the All-Ireland replay, Trevor Giles crucially scored for Meath (Meath 2–09, Mayo 1–11).

1999: Trevor Giles missed a penalty for Meath, but the team still went on to win (Meath 1–11, Cork 1–08).

2001: A Trevor Giles missed penalty seemed to deflate Meath and Galway won by a margin of nine points (Galway 0–17, Meath 0–08).

2002: In the first half Oisin McConville's penalty kick was saved by Kerry's Declan O'Keeffe, but McConville offset this miss with a second-half goal (Armagh 1–12, Kerry 0–14).

Remarkable Players

The only footballer to win All-Ireland medals in a sixty-minute, seventy-minute and eighty-minute final was Brendan Lynch of Kerry: (1969, 60 minutes), (1970, 80 minutes), (1975, 70 minutes).

Patsy Lynch of Cavan, at sixteen years of age, was the youngest player ever to play in an All-Ireland football final (1928).

Mick Doyle of Kerry won four of his All-Ireland Senior Football medals before his twenty-first birthday (1929 to 1932).

The Spillanes, Pat and Tom, from Kerry won nineteen Senior Football medals between them in the years 1975 to 1986.

The only father and son to pick up the Sam Maguire Cup were J. J. Sheehy, who captained Kerry in 1926 and 1930, and his son Seán Óg, who captained the same county in 1962.

Goalkeepers

The role of the goalkeeper evolved after 2000 into more than simply not conceding goals. Traditionally in Gaelic football, when the goalkeeper kicked out the ball the aim would have been to achieve the longest possible distance. However, in the modern game the emphasis is on possession, which means that when a keeper is taking a kick-out he must ensure he gives the ball to a member of his own team. The website Pundit Arena ranks the ten best goalkeepers since 2000 as follows:[7]

Stephen Cluxton (Dublin): An exceptional free-taker particularly remembered for his last-minute free which won the 2011 final. He captained the Dublin team in the victories of 2013, 2015 and 2016. His kick-outs are a very important part of the Dublin strategy.

Paul Durcan (Donegal): Won an All-Star when Donegal won the All-Ireland in 2012.

Pascal McConnell (Tyrone): In goal when Tyrone won in 2005 and 2008.

Fergal Byron (Laois): Winner of an All-Star in 2003.

Gary Connaughton (Westmeath): All-Star in 2008. He also has a European Under-19 Soccer Championship medal.

Alan Quirke (Cork): Played in goal when Cork won the All-Ireland in 2010.

Diarmuid Murphy (Kerry): Won four All-Ireland medals in total.

Paul Hearty (Armagh): One of the most decorated goalkeepers in the twenty-first century, holding nineteen Armagh club football titles and six All-Ireland club titles.

John Devine (Tyrone): Played in Tyrone's first win in 2003.

David Clarke (Mayo): All-Star goalkeeper in 2016.

10

RETURN TO DUNMANWAY ON THE SEVENTY-FIFTH ANNIVERSARY OF THE CUP

To mark the seventy-fifth anniversary of the first presentation of the cup in 1928, all the surviving winning captains were invited to Dunmanway in September 2003. Following a lunch in the Parkway Hotel, a convoy of vintage cars preceded by the Artane Boys Band carried the captains to the market square in the town, where a statue of Sam Maguire had been erected the year before. (The market square is now named Sam Maguire Plaza.) Each captain who was there on the day and representatives of those who had passed away or could not attend were presented with a Waterford Crystal replica of the cup by the then president of the GAA, Seán Kelly.

The event was hosted by RTÉ newsreader Eileen Dunne. Her father, Mick Dunne, had been a noted commentator on all aspects of GAA games. The first presentation was made to a nephew representing Bill (Squire) Gannon, who was the captain of the Kildare team that won the first the Sam Maguire Cup in 1928.

The oldest captain attending was Jimmy Murray (86), who led Roscommon in the double of 1943 and 1944. He sang 'The West's Awake'. This song describes Ireland's long history of successive defeats in the country's struggle for independence from England; however, the final verse strikes a note of hope:

> And if, when all a vigil keep
> The West's asleep, the West's asleep
> Alas! and well may Erin weep
> That Connacht lies in slumber deep.
> But, hark! a voice like thunder spake,
> The West's awake! The West's awake!
> Sing, Oh! hurrah! let England quake,
> We'll watch till death for Erin's sake.

Cork first won the cup in 1945, when the captain was Tadhg Crowley of Clonakilty; he was represented by his niece. The team included local man Éamonn Young, who won a county junior championship with the local club, the Dohenys, in 1966 at the age of forty-eight.

Peter McDermott – 'The Man in the Cap', referee in the 1953 final and captain of the Meath team that won in 1954 – was the second-oldest captain present.

Kevin Heffernan, captain of Dublin in 1958, was unable to be present because of other commitments and was represented by a friend.

Mick O'Connell, captain of Kerry in 1959, was present. The local newspaper reported that he seemed fit enough to play a match.

Kevin Mussen of Down – the first captain to carry the cup across the border to Northern Ireland – also attended.

Des Foley, captain of the 1963 Dublin team, was represented by his wife.

Joe Lennon, captain of Down in 1968, had written a poem in that year which he amended for this occasion. He read his amended version – 'The Parade of Past Captains' – on the day.

Tony McTague, captain of Offaly in the 1972 final, was present.

Then came Billy Morgan, who remembered the final that Cork won in 1973 not only for the glory it brought to his beloved Cork, but also for the battle he had in getting through the thousands of supporters before he reached the dressing room.

Also present was Michael (Mickey Ned) O'Sullivan of

Kerry, who had not been able to accept the cup in 1975 as he was concussed during the game and taken to hospital.

Tony Hanahoe of Dublin recalled some wonderful games against players such as Ogie Moran.

Páidí Ó Sé and Tommy Doyle of Kerry represented the period of Kerry domination in the 1980s before Mick Lyons began a new era for Meath in 1987.

Denis Allen, captain of the victorious 1989 Cork team, was represented by his sister.

Larry Tompkins was another attendee. He had captained Cork in 1990 when they had won back-to-back football finals.

John O'Leary, who led Dublin to victory in 1995, was present. He was followed by Pat McGeeney, father of Kieran McGeeney (who was unable to attend), the captain of the Armagh team that won the cup for the first time in 2002, the year before the seventy-fifth anniversary. The Armagh team were again involved in 2003. Local man John Deane responded to a request from Kieran McGeeney's parents to visit Sam Maguire's home in Mallabracka by driving them to the site.

Tommy Drumm, who led Dublin's 'twelve apostles' to victory against Galway in 1983, spoke on behalf of all the captains who were present.

Finally, GAA president Seán Kelly completed the ceremony. He declared, 'These captains have brought great glory and honour to their counties and families and indeed it would be fitting to say never was there so much happiness brought to so many by so few.' He went on to acknowledge the magnificent contribution from Waterford Crystal, and the contribution made by the various organising bodies that brought about this unique event in the home town of Sam Maguire.

ENDNOTES

1 Dunmanway Youth

1   Mallabracka means 'land of the little hillocks'.
2   Mike Cronin, *Sport and Nationalism in Ireland* (Four Courts Press, 1999), p. 139.
3   The information here is based on the work of Tim Feen of the *Ardfield/ Rathbarry Journal*, 2000–1.
4   www.bbc.com/news/magazine-23376561 (accessed 27 March 2017). Anthony Trollope (1815–1862), the famous English author, is given credit for the introduction of the stand-alone post box in 1852 during his career in the UK Post Office.
5   *Ibid.*
6   *Ibid.*
7   Roy Foster, *Vivid Faces* (Penguin, 2015), pp. 237–38.
8   Tim Pat Coogan, *Michael Collins* (Hutchinson, 1990), p. 14.
9   Barry Attoe, email to author, 21 June 2014.
10 P. S. O'Hegarty, Bureau of Military History (hereafter BMH), Witness Statement (hereafter WS) 840, p. 2.

2 The Irish and the GAA in England

1   Stephen Moore and Paul Darby, *Gaelic Games, Irish Nationalist Politics and the Irish Diaspora in London, 1895–1915* (University of Ulster, 2011), p. 261.
2   *Ibid.*
3   Pat Griffin, *Gaelic Hearts: A History of London GAA, 1896–1996* (London Co. Board Gaelic Athletic Association, 2011), p. 29.
4   *Ibid.*, p. 27.
5   *Ibid.*, p. 61.
6   www.gaa.ie/mm/Document/TheGAA/RulesandRegulations/12/66/5 5/2016OfficialGuide-Part1_English.pdf, p. 1.

3 Sam Maguire's Participation in All-Ireland Finals

1 Eoghan Corry, *History of Gaelic Football* (Gill and Macmillan, 2010), p. 55.
2 *Ibid.*, p. 48.
3 Griffin, *Gaelic Hearts*, p. 63.
4 *The Freeman's Journal,* 27 October 1902.
5 *Ibid.*
6 *The Cork Examiner*, 28 October 1902.
7 Griffin, *Gaelic Hearts*, p. 64.
8 *The Cork Examiner*, 3 August 1903.
9 Griffin, *Gaelic Hearts*, pp. 66–67.
10 *Ibid.*, p. 70.
11 Corry, *History of Gaelic Football*, p. 68.
12 *Ibid.*, pp. 68 and 118.
13 Griffin, *Gaelic Hearts*, p. 8.
14 *Ibid.*, p. 83.
15 *Ibid.*
16 *Kerry Sentinel*, 15 November 1905.
17 Griffin, *Gaelic Hearts*, p. 87.
18 www.nytimes.com/learning/general/onthisday/harp/0930.html (accessed 27 March 2017).
19 Griffin, *Gaelic Hearts*, p. 87.
20 *Ibid.*

4 Sam Maguire's Work for the Republican Cause in London

1 http://the1916proclamation.ie (accessed 4 April 2017).
2 Dr Brian A. Cusack, BMH WS 736, p. 1.
3 Roger Swift and Sheridan Gilley (eds), *The Irish in Britain 1815–1939* (Barnes and Noble, 1989), p. 35.
4 *Ibid.*
5 *Ibid.*
6 Coogan, *Michael Collins*, p. 16.
7 Peter Hart, *Mick* (Macmillan, 2006), p. 55.
8 P. S. O'Hegarty, BMH WS 847, p. 1.
9 Gerard Noonan, *The IRA in Britain, 1919–1923: 'In the Heart of Enemy Lines'* (Liverpool University Press, 2014), p. 44.

10 Peter Hart, *The I.R.A. at War 1916–1923* (Oxford University Press, 2003), p. 146.

11 Elizabeth McGinley, BMH WS 860, pp. 2–3.

12 Quoted in Griffin, *Gaelic Hearts*, p. 165.

13 For the complete story see John Gaynor, BMH WS 1447, pp. 3–8.

14 Piaras Béaslaí quoted in Frank Thornton, BMH WS 615, pp. 10–11.

15 Elizabeth McGinley, BMH WS 860, p. 2.

16 Richard Walsh, IRB and Mayo IRA, BMH WS 400, p. 130.

17 Joe Dolan, BMH WS 900, p. 8.

18 Richard Walsh, BMH WS 400, pp. 137–38.

19 *Ibid.*, pp. 139–40.

20 James Delaney, BMH WS 1360, pp. 1–5.

21 Richard Walsh, BMH WS 400, p. 65.

22 Pa Murray, BMH WS 1584, p. 18.

23 *Ibid.*

24 *Ibid.*, pp. 19–20.

25 *Ibid.*, p. 20.

26 *Ibid.*

27 George Fitzgerald, BMH WS 684, pp. 28–30.

28 *Ibid.*, p. 30.

29 Hugh Early, BMH WS 1535, pp. 2–4.

30 *Ibid.*, p. 8.

31 Frank Thornton, BMH WS 615, p. 29.

32 *Ibid.*, p. 30.

33 *Ibid.*, pp. 30–31.

34 Tom Barry, *Guerilla Days in Ireland* (Irish Press, 1949), p. 27.

35 Ted Hayes, BMH WS 1575, p. 6.

36 Frank Thornton, BMH WS 615, p. 47.

37 *Ibid.*, p. 48.

38 *Ibid.*, pp. 38–39.

39 Joseph Kinsella, BMH WS 476, pp. 15–16.

40 David Neligan, BMH WS 380, p. 4.

41 Daniel Healy, BMH WS 1656, p. 13.

42 *Ibid.*, pp. 15–16.

43 Noonan, *The IRA in Britain, 1919–1923*, p. 46.

44 www.irishtimes.com/opinion/opinion-constitutional-means-would-not-have-delivered-self-determination-in-1916-1.2501240 (accessed

27 March 2017).

45 www.irishstatutebook.ie/eli/1922/act/1/schedule/2/enacted/en/html (accessed 27 March 2017).

46 "'This Splendid Historic Organisation": The Irish Republican Brotherhood among the Anti-Treatyites, 1921–4', www.theirishstory.com/2015/04/27/this-splendid-historic-organisation-the-irish-republican-brotherhood-among-the-anti-treatyites-1921-4/#.WN619lUrKM (accessed 4 April 2017).

47 Vincent MacDowell, *Michael Collins and the IRB* (Ashfield Press, 1997), p. 117.

48 Joe Dolan, BMH WS 900, p. 2.

49 *Ibid.*, pp. 2–4.

50 *Ibid.*, pp. 4–5.

5   Return to Dublin and Dismissal

1 P. S. O'Hegarty, BMH WS 897, p. 2.

2 Griffin, *Gaelic Hearts*, p. 132.

3 Dáil Debates, Adjournment Debate – Dismissal of a Civil Servant, 13 May 1926, see http://oireachtasdebates.oireachtas.ie/debates%20authoring/debateswebpack.nsf/takes/dail1926051300028?opendocument (accessed 27 March 2017).

4 Barry Attoe, email to author, 21 June 2014.

5 John Bowyer Bell, *The Secret Army* (Sphere Books, 1972), p. 62.

6 John M. Regan, *The Irish Counter-Revolution, 1921–1936* (St Martin's Press, 1999), p. 196.

7 Elizabeth McGinley, BMH WS 860, pp. 2–3.

8 Cabinet file on the dismissal of Sam Maguire, reference S7673, National Archives of Ireland.

9 *Ibid.*

10 *Ibid.*

11 *Ibid.*

12 *Ibid.*

13 *Ibid.*

14 Elizabeth McGinley, BMH WS 860, p. 3. It seems that Maguire was staying with his friend Bob O'Kennedy at 112 Pembroke Road, Dublin 4.

15 Dáil Debates, Ceisteanna – Questions. Oral Answers. – Dismissed

Civil Servant, 12 May 1926, see http://oireachtasdebates.oireachtas.ie/
debates%20authoring/debateswebpack.nsf/takes/dail1926051200003?
opendocument (accessed 27 March 2017).

16 Dáil Debates, Adjournment Debate – Dismissal of a Civil Servant,
13 May 1926, see http://oireachtasdebates.oireachtas.ie/debates%20
authoring/debateswebpack.nsf/takes/dail1926051300028?open
document (accessed 27 March 2017).

17 *Ibid.*

18 *Ibid.*

19 *Ibid.*

20 *Ibid.*

6 Death

1 *Irish Independent*, 9 February 1927.

2 *The Southern Star*, 5 March 1927.

3 *Ibid.*

7 Creation of the Sam Maguire Cup

1 'The Illustrious Sam Maguire', *An tÓglách*, vol. 1, no. 10, Easter 1965.

2 'Dunmanway Notes', *The Southern Star*, 19 March 1927.

3 Kevin C. Kearns, *Dublin Pub Life and Lore: An Oral History* (Roberts
Rinehart Publishers, 1997), p. 40.

4 Cabinet file on the dismissal of Sam Maguire, reference S7673,
National Archives of Ireland.

5 *The Southern Star*, 31 March 1928.

6 Corry, *History of Gaelic Football*, p. 119.

7 Minutes, GAA central committee meeting, 3 December 1927, GAA
Archive, Croke Park, Dublin.

8 *Leinster Leader*, 6 October 1928.

8 Significant Moments in the History of the All-Ireland Finals

1 Corry, *History of Gaelic Football*, p. 121.

2 *The Irish Times*, 6 May 2006: Keith Duggan interview with Jimmy
Murray, the man who captained Roscommon to their first All-Ireland
senior football title in 1943.

3 John Scally, *The GAA: An Oral History* (Mainstream, 2009).

4   www.terracetalk.com/articles/Memories/70/The-1946-All-Ireland-Final-and-the-Antrim-Objection (accessed 28 March 2017).

5   www.anfearrua.com/topic.aspx?id=671201 (accessed 28 March 2017).

6   Quoted in Brendan O'Brien, 'The Greatest Decider of them All', *Irish Examiner*, 15 September 2007, see www.irishexaminer.com/ireland/the-greatest-decider-of-them-all-42636.html (accessed 28 March 2017).

7   http://gaa.eir.ie/experience-speaks/2013/07/24/cavans-foreign-quests; www.irishtimes.com/sport/kerry-shine-in-the-big-apple-1.117501 (accessed 28 March 2017).

8   'Unbreakable Bond Still Echoes Down the Airwaves', *Irish Independent*, 24 December 2006, www.independent.ie/sport/unbreakable-bond-still-echoes-down-the-airwaves-26420099.html (accessed 4 April 2017).

9   www.seamusjking.com/Articles%20Full/football.html (accessed 4 April 2017).

10 www.sportsjoe.ie/gaa/hill-16-was-named-after-a-turkish-battle-not-the-easter-rising-40331 (accessed 4 April 2017).

11 www.historyireland.com/20th-century-contemporary-history/the-1956-polio-epidemic-in-cork/ (accessed 28 March 2017).

12 Mick O'Connell, *A Kerry Footballer* (Mercier Press, 1974), p. 64.

13 www.terracetalk.com/articles/Brendan-O-Sullivan/229/Mick-Oconnell (accessed 28 March 2017).

14 *Ibid.*

15 Dónal McAnallen, *The Story of Gaelic Games in Ulster* (Cardinal Tomás Ó Fiaich Memorial Library & Archive, 2010), p. 22.

16 Diarmuid O'Donovan, 'Lessons from the All-Ireland Football Final', www.dodonovan.com/?p=642 (accessed 4 April 2017).

17 Gabriel Fitzmaurice, *In Praise of Football* (Mercier Press, 2009).

18 Quoted in Sean Kilfeather, 'No Rest for the Boys of '67', *The Irish Times*, 12 September 1996.

19 Corry, *History of Gaelic Football*, p. 226.

20 *The Irish Times*, 29 September 1969.

21 www.terracetalk.com/articles/569/Tribute-to-Din-Joe-Crowley (accessed 28 March 2017).

22 http://kerrygaa.proboards.com/thread/6520/rip-den-joe-crowley#ixzz4d7S5HqAQ (accessed 4 April 2017).

23 Corry, *History of Gaelic Football*, p. 230.

24 *The Irish Times*, 28 June 2014.

25 www.the42.ie/the-history-boys-dublin-versus-cork-125024-Apr2011/ (accessed 28 March 2017).

26 www.irishtimes.com/sport/gaelic-games/gaelic-football/forty-years-a-growing-dublin-football-s-rise-from-obscurity-1.1848246 (accessed 28 March 2017).

27 Corry, *History of Gaelic Football*, p. 249.

28 www.rte.ie/sport/gaa/2015/0918/728764-dublin-v-kerry-a-football-rivalry (accessed 28 March 2017).

29 http://politico.ie/archive/odwyers-kingdom; http://www.seamusjking. com/Articles%20Full/football.html (accessed 28 March 2017).

30 www.rte.ie/sport/gaa/2015/0918/728764-dublin-v-kerry-a-football-rivalry (accessed 28 March 2017).

31 Mitchell Cogley, *Irish Independent*, 23 August 1977.

32 Joe Joyce, *The Irish Times*, 25 September 1978; see also www.rte.ie/ sport/gaa/2015/0918/728764-dublin-v-kerry-a-football-rivalry (accessed 4 April 2017).

33 *The Irish Press*, 20 September 2015.

34 'Stars of Mikey's "Greatest Freak of All Time" Reunite at Austin Stacks Lunch', *Tralee Today*, 25 February 2017, http://traleetoday. ie/stars-mikeys-greatest-freak-time-reunite-austin-stacks-lunch (accessed 4 April 2017).

35 Declan Lynch, personal communication to author, March 2017.

36 www.terracetalk.com/articles/Memories/22/The-Goal-that-Rocked-a-Kingdom (accessed 28 March 2017).

37 *Sunday World*, 19 September 1982.

38 Michael Foley, *Kings of September* (O'Brien Press, 2007).

39 'Summer of 83', *Irish Independent*, 22 January 2017, www.independent. ie/sport/gaelic-football/summer-of-83-26469498.html (accessed 28 March 2017).

40 *The Irish Times*, 18 September 2015.

41 www.wearedublin.com/football/kevin-heffernans-famous-words-to-his-dublin-team-before-the-84-all-ireland-semi-final (accessed 4 April 2017).

42 www.balls.ie/gaa/balls-remembers-dublins-unwise-open-topped-bus-parade-1992-136113 (accessed 28 March 2017).

43 *Ibid.*

44 *Irish Examiner*, 24 August 2011.

45 'Fans Rescued', *Irish Independent*, 20 September 1993.

46 *Irish Independent*, 7 August 2005.

47 'Pat McEnaney: "I went from being the best referee in Ireland to worst. All in a week"', www.irishtimes.com/sport/gaelic-games/gaelic-football/pat-mcenaney-i-went-from-being-the-best-referee-in-ireland-to-worst-all-in-a-week-1.2810893 (accessed 20 June 2017).

48 Corry, *History of Gaelic Football*, p. 314.

49 'Croker Rout as Kerry go Heavy on Mayo', *Irish Independent*, 27 September 2004.

50 'Kingdom use their know-how to squeeze life out of the Rebels', *Irish Independent*, 21 September 2009.

51 'Dublin Ends 16 Years of Hurt as Heroic Fightback sends Capital into Ecstasy', www.independent.ie/sport/gaelic-football/dublin-end-16-years-of-hurt-as-heroic-fightback-sends-capital-into-ecstasy-26773161.html (accessed 28 March 2017).

52 Coppers: a Dublin pub and nightclub.

53 'All-Ireland Final 2012: Donegal rise to seize their day', *Belfast Telegraph*, 24 September 2012, www.belfasttelegraph.co.uk/sport/gaa/allireland-final-2012-donegal-rise-to-seize-their-day-28866486.html (accessed 28 March 2017).

9   Sam Maguire Cup Miscellany of Facts and Figures

1   www.balls.ie/gaa/343410-343410 (accessed 20 June 2017).

2   *Ibid.*

3   All of these players bar Declan Browne were listed in Liam Kelly, 'Best Players of 21st Century Never to Win an All-Ireland', *Irish Independent*, 22 December 2014.

4   Corry, *History of Gaelic Football*, p. 306.

5   www.gaa.ie/the-gaa/rules-regulations (accessed 28 March 2017).

6   Corry, *History of Gaelic Football*, p. 306.

7   www.punditarena.com/gaa/smurphy/gaelic-football-ten-best-goalkeepers-since-2010 (accessed 28 March 2017).

BIBLIOGRAPHY

Archives
British Postal Museum & Archive (www.archives.gov/research/post-offices)
Bureau of Military History, Dublin (www.bureauofmilitaryhistory.ie)
GAA Archive, Croke Park, Dublin
Irish Newspaper Archive (www.irishnewsarchive.com)
National Archives of Ireland, Bishop Street, Dublin

Books
Barry, Tom, *Guerilla Days in Ireland* (Irish Press, 1949)
Bowyer Bell, John, *The Secret Army* (Sphere Books, 1972)
Coogan, Tim Pat, *Michael Collins: A Biography* (Hutchinson, 1990)
Corry, Eoghan, *History of Gaelic Football* (Gill and Macmillan, 2010)
Cronin, Mike, *Sport and Nationalism in Ireland* (Four Courts Press, 1999)
Fitzmaurice, Gabriel, *In Praise of Football* (Mercier Press, 2009)
Foley, Michael, *Kings of September* (O'Brien Press, 2007)
Foster, Roy, *Vivid Faces* (Penguin, 2015)
Griffin, Pat, *Gaelic Hearts: A History of London GAA, 1896–1996* (London
    Co. Board Gaelic Athletic Association, 2011)
Hart, Peter, *The I.R.A. at War 1916–1923* (Oxford University Press, 2003)
Hart, Peter, *Mick* (Macmillan, 2006)
Kearns, Kevin C., *Dublin Pub Life and Lore: An Oral History* (Roberts
    Rinehart Publishers, 1997)
MacDowell, Vincent, *Michael Collins and the IRB* (Ashfield Press, 1997)
McAnallen, Dónal, *The Story of Gaelic Games in Ulster* (Cardinal Tomás Ó
    Fiaich Memorial Library & Archive, 2010)

Moore, Stephen and Darby, Paul, *Gaelic Games, Irish Nationalist Politics and the Irish Diaspora in London, 1895–1915* (University of Ulster, 2011)

Noonan, Gerard, *The IRA in Britain, 1919–1923: 'In the Heart of Enemy Lines'* (Liverpool University Press, 2014)

O'Connell, Mick, *A Kerry Footballer* (Mercier Press, 1974)

Regan, John M., *The Irish Counter-Revolution, 1921–1936* (St Martin's Press, 1999)

Rouse, Paul, *Sport and Ireland: A History* (Oxford University Press, 2015)

Scalley, John, *The GAA: An Oral History* (Mainstream, 2009)

Swift, Roger, and Gilley, Sheridan (eds), *The Irish in Britain 1815–1939* (Barnes and Noble, 1989)

Websites

http://gaa.eir.ie/experience-speaks/2013/07/24/cavans-foreign-quests

http://kerrygaa.proboards.com/thread/6520/rip-den-joe-crowley#ixzz 4d7S5HqAQ

http://oireachtasdebates.oireachtas.ie

http://politico.ie/archive/odwyers-kingdom

http://the1916proclamation.ie

http://traleetoday.ie/stars-mikeys-greatest-freak-time-reunite-austin-stacks-lunch

www.anfearrua.com/topic.aspx?id=671201

www.balls.ie/gaa/balls-remembers-dublins-unwise-open-topped-bus-parade-1992-136113

www.bbc.com/news/magazine-23376561

www.belfasttelegraph.co.uk/sport/gaa/allireland-final-2012-donegal-rise-to-seize-their-day-28866486.html

www.dodonovan.com/?p=642

www.gaa.ie

www.historyireland.com/20th-century-contemporary-history/the-1956-polio-epidemic-in-cork/

www.independent.ie

www.irishexaminer.com/ireland/the-greatest-decider-of-them-all-42636.
html

www.irishstatutebook.ie/eli/1922/act/1/schedule/2/enacted/en/html

www.irishtimes.com

www.nytimes.com/learning/general/onthisday/harp/0930.html

www.punditarena.com/gaa/smurphy/gaelic-football-ten-best-goalkeepers-
since-2010

www.rte.ie/sport/gaa/2015/0918/728764-dublin-v-kerry-a-football-rivalry

www.seamusjking.com/Articles%20Full/football.html

www.sportsjoe.ie/gaa/hill-16-was-named-after-a-turkish-battle-not-the-
easter-rising-40331

www.terracetalk.com

www.the42.ie/the-history-boys-dublin-versus-cork-125024-Apr2011

www.theirishstory.com/2015/04/27/this-splendid-historic-organisation-
the-irish-republican-brotherhood-among-the-anti-treatyites-1921-4/#.
WN6l9lUrKM

www.wearedublin.com/football/kevin-heffernans-famous-words-to-his-
dublin-team-before-the-84-all-ireland-semi-final

INDEX